THE ANATOMY OF SPORTS FANS

Reflections on Fans & Fanatics

PIERRE D. BOGNON

ISBN: 1-4392-1037-3
ISBN-13: 9781439210376
Library of Congress Control Number: 2008908325

Visit www.booksurge.com to order additional copies..

PREAMBLE

Sport is the language spoken by all the men in our family. We talk soccer, football, or anything that is competitive and in season. It is the topic of our conversations when we are reunited after a long separation. For our friends, sport references are often passwords to intimacy. Being fans brings us together. It puts us all on an equal footing, all with access to the same knowledge and emotions. We are but a small sample of the world of sport fans.

We have often asked ourselves why we identify with one team or another, become so passionate when it is competing, and sink into a depression when it loses a game.

This is how the idea for this book was born.

This project had an added twist. "Fan" is derived from "fanatic," and it can be assumed that the two terms have more in common than their etymology. The same road might lead a man to becoming a fanatic or a fan; the reasons for his strong identification and uncompromising behavior might be similar.

Understanding the world of fans might help us learn something about fanatics. Sport fans are not shy in acknowledging their excesses, they readily admit that they cannot shed or control their fanhood. Fanatics show no such moments of lucidity. Don't men talk a lot about sport to stay away from the minefields of religion, politics, and ideologies?

I looked for sources of information on both sides of the Atlantic, visited libraries, talked to fans, and tried to become familiar with the contributions of scholars to this topic.

During the many years that it took to finalize this project I have been constantly prodded by my daughters and have relied on the know-how of my son, sons-in-law and their friend, J.T, the "professional" fans.

How my son Nicholas became a true fan is recounted in this book. Derek, my American son-in-law, grew up in the shadow of the teams from Boston and built upon that foundation to become an all-around sport fan. Tim, my English son-in -law, set aside his love for cricket and rugby when he moved to the U.S and became one of the boys by learning to speak baseball and football.

My wife, a typical representative of those who take pride in their lack of interest in institutional sport, the "out-group," was always a step ahead of me when the topic was psychology or sociology. She has been my favorite editor.

❊ ❊ ❊

INTRODUCTION

At dusk on the evening of June 5, 1944, General Eisenhower drove to the airfield at Newbury, England, where the 101st Airborne Division was about to embark on C 47's to be parachuted over occupied France. Its participation in the Normandy invasion had been so severely questioned by RAF Air Marshall Trafford Leigh-Mallory that it had been labeled "the futile slaughter."

Early that very morning, Ike had made the call to start Operation Overlord the next day, June 6, and his meeting with these soldiers has been preserved for posterity by numerous photographs. These show young men, a smile illuminating their blackened faces, and the General among them, a hand in his pocket. There are various accounts of the conversations that took place. In one of them the General asked "And you, where are you from?" Numerous states were represented: Georgia, Kansas, Texas. They talked about fishing and sports. The name of a college team would have belonged naturally in the conversations: Bulldogs, Jayhawks, Longhorns. The quick exchanges between fans or archrivals created a bond between them, a comfort on the eve of moments so crucial in the life of Ike and fatal for many of these young soldiers. This is one of my favorite scenes involving sport fandom. It reminds us that it is a world of common experiences which brings men together (Note 1) (Notes mentioned in each chapter will be found at the end of that chapter).

Another much less dramatic and more personal story will illustrate how sport is a common language for men and a world apart for its fans. In the 1980's, my wife and I took a train from Chihuahua, Mexico, through the spectacular Barranca del Cobre (Copper Canyon) to the end of the line along the Pacific coast in Los Mochis. In the evening, we strolled through the Zocalo and heard the unmistakable sound of a televised soccer game, the high pitch, the speedy delivery, all in the vein of the "Goll!!!" now so familiar to soccer fans around the world. I did not resist the temptation, entered the bar, but stayed in a no man's land. My reactions to the action on the TV screen caught the attention of three "fans." They sensed my understanding of soccer, waved at me to join them, and we shared a few cervezas while excitedly commenting on the game. I was no longer a gringo but had become a compadre. At the end of the game, they invited me to join them for a night out in town to celebrate the victory of "our team" and promised to take me back to my hotel. This was not to be. We had indulged in our common passion, but my wife made sure that I remembered that when the game stops reality takes over.

Some readers will relate to these stories and recall their own experiences; others will feel largely unconcerned. The world is split when the topic is sport and its fandom. Members of the "in-group" range from enthusiastic to excessively passionate and even obsessive. Those who form the "out-group" show little interest but are not virulent in their opposition. My daughter Claire has learned to graciously organize her evenings around Mets games, her English husband's favorite baseball team, even though she remains immune to the excitement of these events. Most are proud of their indifference and look down on the avid readers of the sports section in the daily paper or the sports pages on the internet.

Both groups are puzzled by the same questions. They wonder why sport fans are held spellbound by the sight of a soccer ball crisscrossing the field for ninety minutes or more without a goal being scored. They ask why college and high school students, abandoning all civility, invade football fields and tear down goalposts. True fans wonder why they are addicted to sport in general or some sport in particular. They try to understand why they cannot shed their apparently irrational attachment to a team and seem unable to control their emotions when it is competing. In support of their perplexity, the fans in my family talk about how my father-in-law, a neurosurgeon, became physically ill when the Michigan Wolverines were losing to Ohio State, or recall how a French friend of my son, at the age of twenty-seven, cried when France beat Brazil in the final of the 1998 Soccer World Cup.

Academic research should be a reliable source of information on sports fans, their motivations, behavior, and role in society, but social scientists claim that they don't know enough. In *Theorizing Fandom, Fans, Subculture and Identity*, a book written in 1998, Cheryl Harris and Alison Alexander tell us that: "Fans and their social and cultural environment are untheorized in social sciences; we know virtually nothing about what produces fandom, what role they play in social and cultural processes." In *Sport Fans, the Psychological and Social Impact of Spectators*, the authors, led by Daniel L. Wann, the Murray State University professor of psychology, discuss the state of psychological and sociological research and theory on sport fandom at the end of 2000. They conclude that sport is pervasive in society and a major component of modern life but that there is a lack of research about its fans.

This is still fairly true in 2008 despite a large body of academic work on several aspects of sport fandom. The favorite subject is spectator aggression in its multiple manifestations; social values such as "sport fandom and national identity" are also well researched. Statistical analyses on the sources of identification are available, but most of these, unfortunately, have only been done with samples of college students.

Many reasons can be cited for the relative lack of interest that sport fandom generates. It is still a new topic, not well-delineated, with overlaps between the study of the importance of sport and the social role of its spectators and its fans. People who do not care about sport are not inclined to learn about its fans. The reputation of sport fans is mostly negative, and this does not make for an attractive topic of research. I can testify to the lack of general interest. Since I started this book, I have explained my project to "non-fans" and casual fans on numerous occasions and have faced the same reaction every time: a look of surprise, an expression of disbelief difficult to suppress, and a studied form of enthusiasm after I had explained the theme and its relationship with identity, fanaticism, and the human condition.

The writings of fans about themselves and what has been written about groups of fans are rich sources of information. Many entertaining books are readily available. In *Rammer, Jammer, Yellow Hammer*, Warren St. John dissects the idiosyncrasies of those University of Alabama Crimson Tide football fans who travel in their RVs from game to game. Tim Parks, in *A Season in Verona*, takes the reader through the madness surrounding soccer games in Italy. Both authors have spent a whole season with a team, and this allows for an intimate understanding of their fans. *Fever Pitch* by Nick Hornby is the archetypical memoir of a sport fan. He has been obsessed with the London soccer team called Arsenal ever since he first saw it play when he was eleven years old. I have borrowed the title of Chapter 3: "Why has the relationship that began as a schoolboy crush endured for nearly a quarter century…?" from his book. Ex-hooligans have been very prolific, and many autobiographies are on the shelves of bookstores in England.

There are newspaper and magazine articles mostly on the dark side of sport fandom and usually published after cases of excessive rowdiness at a college stadium or violence at some soccer game.

Sport is an unending inspiration for filmmakers. A favorite theme is the underdog whose perseverance wins the day. Fans are mostly in the background; *The Fan*, staring Robert de Niro, is a rare case where they take center stage.

An ever renewable source is the Internet, where thousands of sites contain the keywords "sport fan." This is a truly global resource, a compendium of news and stories about clubs and athletes in all sports and on all continents. On "Google," these sites, mostly classified by popularity, give a picture of the centers of interest of sport fans. During the period 2003–2007, a heavy dose was devoted to specific teams and another large number to discussion forums, social networking, and message boards. Fantasy teams seem more and more to capture the imagination of fans. All in all, the Internet is an instructive introduction to the world of sport fans, their profile, and motivations. Some searches have yielded amusing results. At the London City Barbican Library the keyword "fan" brings references of several recordings of *Cosi fan Tutte*. Mozart didn't know that in the world of googling his (sexist!) opera would end up next to books on hooligans.

The observation of and discussions with fans provided the best information and were the most fun to gather. There are plenty of them around, and they are not reluctant to share their experiences. It allows for an understanding of the origin of their fanhood and, most importantly, an insight into how they live their obsession. They offer rich material for entertaining stories, and I have enjoyed using some to illustrate my reflections. I have done this with parsimony, though, because my goal was to go beyond the description of the behavior of fans and address the "why," to search for answers to questions such as how they became fans, why they stay so committed, and if the process says something about the human psyche?

One major theme emerged from these sources. Fans belong to a community which can be a source of identity. Sports offer possibilities of socializing by joining groups which some sociologists (Michel Maffesoli, to name but one, who wrote *Le Temps des Tribus* in 1988) call "tribes." Their members come together to support "their" team when they gather in a bar or form large crowds in a stadium, and they share a "psychological space" when they are geographically dispersed. Most become highly animated watching a competition, but when the game is over, resume their day-to-day activities without psychological scars. Others, the real fans, have found in these tribes a source of identity. They might have become members as a result of fortuitous events which took place usually during their adolescence or by their own choice. In any case, once branded by a team or athlete, they cannot escape their identification. They are exhilarated by victories and spend emotional energy to protect their image when it is threatened by poor performance.

Other leisure activities allow people to feel connected. They can join aficionados of movie stars, rock singers, or even opera "divas." Members of all fan tribes have similar behavior patterns. Sports fans, though, are the most excessive. This is the result of the high level of tension generated by sport competitions. No spectator can doubt that they are exhilarating experiences. These events, unscripted but with a definite outcome, are a constant source of enthusiasm.

Throughout this book I will make numerous references to "enthusiasm." There is a historical connection between enthusiasm and fanaticism and, as a result, with fandom. During the 18th century, members of religious sects, who today would be called fanatics, were labeled enthusiasts. These believers were convinced that they had the truth, that they were, as indicated by the etymology of enthusiast, "possessed by a god." Today, the word has lost most of its religious connotation but has kept its implication of excess. It defines man sharing his feelings and reaching for others, transcending himself. It is generally associated with physical manifestation of emotions and passions and, in that sense, is well adapted to describe the behavior of a sports fan. When Aristotle writes in part 8 of chapter 5 of *Politics* "enthusiasm is an affection of the soul which strongly agitates the disposition," he seems to have in mind what fans feel at the ball park.

Men also socialize and find sources of identity by joining groups which endorse an ideological, religious, or political cause. Members of such communities share beliefs about things that matter to men. This is why they are not referred to as "fans" belonging to "tribes." Most are passionate, but some can be excessive in their behavior and intransigent with their creed. They can be fanatics.

Developing an understanding of fanaticism is a taller order than dissecting the motivations of fans and describing their behavior. Here, knowledge is not acquired by interviewing those representing fanatical groups or relying on the internet and "googling," but by reaching for the contribution of scholars. The history of fanaticism overlaps that of excessive religious zeal and revolutionary and nationalist mass movements. Real fanatics have intrigued philosophers, sociologists, and psychoanalysts from Voltaire to Koestler to Jung.

Learning about fanatics brings to light that fans and fanatics share major features. They are members of tribes or groups which satisfy their need to belong, and their cause is to fanatics what their team is to fans; it can be a source of identity. This makes the relationship between belonging and identity one of the building blocks of this book.

The first chapter addresses the question of man's need to belong. It gives a cursory, theoretical, and pragmatic view of identity because understanding the making of an identity is fundamental to understanding the unconditional identifications of fans and fanatics. The catalysts which can cause the life-long attachment of a sport fan can also trigger his affiliation with a cause. One of the differences between fans and fanatics is that fans invest energy in things that are not vital to human life and this frees them to speak about their obstinacy.

The anatomy of sports fans begins with Chapter 2 which describes how one becomes a fan and why the identification with a sport/team can remain strong throughout a lifetime. It is, in most cases, the result of events that took place during adolescence. In adulthood, fans become protective of what has branded their identity. How can they be unfaithful to the sport/team which entered their life when they were adolescents?

The next three chapters are a gradual introduction to the world of sport.

The history of institutionalized sports, and particularly team sports, is rather recent. Chapter 3 relates how "fair play" and organized competitions evolved out of free-for-all games after the middle of the 19th century and how the drafting of sets of rules for each sport made competitions possible. Sport offers its fans numerous opportunities for belonging. At the beginning of the 21st century, it is the dominant form of popular culture. This chapter also addresses the question: is sport a religion?

Institutionalized sports have become a major business. Chapter 4 reviews the impact of this evolution on fans. Sports belong in the world of entertainment. This gives athletes and owners access to large sums of money and to a quasi-worldwide market. Many teams are on a par, and this makes for exciting competitions. It is good for spectators and fans, but athletes, who have so much at stake, succumb more and more to their dark sides. The use of performance-enhancing drugs is the best known form of cheating. The clean and polished image that sport cherishes is constantly at risk of being tarnished and the fidelity of its fandom tested. Despite these and other pitfalls, institutionalized sport is a growing business, and its fandom is resilient.

Sports events are singled out from other leisure activites by how enthusiasm is expressed. Chapter 5 builds upon Norbert Elias's theory that they allow a de-controlling of human emotions in a controlled environment. Sports competitions are a source of intense emotions, and spectators can let their bodies and voices express their enthusiasm. This is in contrast to most other leisure activities. The requirement for listeners to control their bodies and voices is evident in concert halls, at the opera, theater or the ballet and is a byproduct of the rise of the bourgeoisie in the 19th century.

The next two chapters are devoted to the behavior of fans. Chapter 6 focuses on the Highly Identified Fans, the HIF, and how they react to glorious victories and devastating defeats. Chapter 7 introduces elements of crowd psychology relevant to fandom. At sports events, fans are part of crowds, and this influences their attitudes. These crowds exhibit two main types of behavior: the Carnival, boisterous but mostly sociable, and the Hooligan, violent and demonizing. There is an often debated issue of whether sport is a place for "blowing off steam" or if it stimulates aggressive behavior. The case is made that even though sport might stimulate the aggressive traits of its spectators, fans who become aggressive are those who find violence generally rewarding. This chapter draws its inspiration from both sides of the Atlantic, so, as one might expect, it addresses the question of why U.S. fan groups have not adopted the Hooligan culture of some of their alter egos in Europe and particularly in England.

The anatomy of sports fans confirms the assumption that fans and fanatics follow similar roads and Chapter 8 is devoted to other manifestations of fanaticism. The word "fanatic" has negative connotations because it is mainly associated with zealots and intransigent people. It also applies, though, to people who are excessively enthusiastic and passionate. Fans exhibiting too much intensity in their identification with a team/athlete show a fanatic tendency. Men who achieved great discoveries, pursued daring explorations, and produced masterpieces were driven by inextinguishable fires. These passionate people who expanded the boundaries of human understanding exhibited fanatic traits in the intensity and excessiveness of their behavior. There is a fine line separating them from the real fanatics, who are overprotective of their creeds, and from the "true believers," who are lead by their belief in absolute truths to dehumanize "the others." That line is usually crossed when a man's faith is no longer informed by his reason. How men of faith become fanatics can be traced to how their identity was formed and how they manage it. This chapter ends with general considerations on a form of fanaticism called terrorism.

The main themes of the book are brought together in the Concluding Remarks. The words "fan" and "fanatic" mostly bring to mind the destructiveness of hooligans at soccer games and the dangerous intransigence of ideological and religious true believers, but at their core, fandom and fanaticism are sources of identity, belonging, and passion. All three are needed to give meaning to our lives. Sports fans find them in their "for its own sake" world. Becoming a fan might be the best first step to fill the emptiness of some people's lives.

NOTE 1

"Sport" and "sports" are not used interchangeably. The singular represents the general concept; the plural is used when several "sports" are involved.

"Man" and "men" are not gender specific; they mean human being(s) unless the context indicates otherwise.

CHAPTER 1

"Mankind never lives completely in the present because identity perpetuates the past."
Sigmund Freud.

The research done on fans and fanatics leads to the question of man's need to socialize and then to the relationship between how he socializes and the makeup of his identity.

THE NEED TO BELONG

It is commonly believed that there is no "I" without "you" and that we are meant to live with others. Eminent philosophers, though, have argued that socializing is not necessary to man. A book by Tzvetan Todorov called *La Vie Commune* presents the rich history of the social dimension of men in a condensed and easily accessible form. Todorov, who was born in Bulgaria and immigrated to France at the age of twenty-four, always felt uprooted and, in the 1970's, was called "the apostle of humanism." Not surprisingly, his views are grounded in his personal history and reflect his humanism.

His book gives an overview of the major trends starting with the moralists during the classical period. Montaigne and La Bruyere considered that man seeks to be acknowledged out of vanity, but his true ideal is to be solitary. Machiavelli and, after the Renaissance, Hobbes, present man as egoistic and in competition with others; society imposes rules on individuals who are essentially solitary and searching for power. Kant's man is torn between his need for the presence of others and his drive for domination and honors which he does not want to share. As is well known, Nietzsche also presents man as seeking to dominate. The paradox of these asocial theories is that whatever man's social nature he needs to impose his will upon others, and he needs them to witness and acknowledge his glory.

Todorov then presents Jean Jacques Rousseau's message that man needs others. On the face of it, there is nothing revolutionary in this except that Rousseau viewed this need to socialize not as an expression of vanity but a defining feature of mankind. Man is incomplete without the presence of others. This is reflected in *The Discourse on Inequality*, which he wrote for an essay contest sponsored by the City of Geneva in 1754. His sweeping history of mankind, starting with the noble savage and ending with a civilized man entangled in a web of social relationships, concludes that, "...the savage lives within himself while social man lives outside himself and can only live in the opinion of others, so that he seems to receive the feeling of his own existence only from the judgment of others." Judgment, here, has the meaning of acknowledgment; to be acknowledged is to exist.

Let's conclude this overview by mentioning that classical psychoanalysis presents man as egoistic and solitary.

Does man need others only to satisfy his vanity and impulses of power and dominance? Is he forced into ties with others because of an ever-growing web of economic interactions? Or, alternatively, is it a feature of mankind to be attracted to others?

For Todorov the answer to "Does man need to belong?" is best found by putting aside philosophical arguments and observing that the very existence of man is tied to the presence of others. Man, a product of society, realizes his true identity only in community. Peter Berger, the Austrian-born, American-educated sociologist and Lutheran theologian, writes in *The Secret Canopy* (1967) that the individual becomes that which he is addressed as by others.

These positions have strong empirical support. It is well known that radical separation from the social world or anomie constitutes a powerful threat to the individual. Senator McCain, recollecting his prison time in Vietnam, confides that the most difficult torture to bear was solitary confinement. It might not break his body, but it could destroy his self. Social neuroscientists believe that the human brain is "wired to connect." The observations of ethologues provide multiple examples of primates living in communities, not only for food gathering, protection, or breeding but for the apparent reason of being together. Evolutionists draw on these observations to defend the view that man is a social being. The English poet-writer John Donne had expressed this thought when he wrote in 1624 the forever famous lines: "No man is an island…any man's death diminishes me…and therefore never send to know for whom the bell tolls."

In the Western world today, most people endorse the view that they are meant to live in the company of their fellow human beings. This is a feature of their society. The context in which they connect has been influenced by their "civilizing process" and the progress in communication technology which is evolving as I write.

The Internet has opened numerous opportunities for joining groups online to share business or cultural interests. In the updated 2006 edition of *The World is Flat*, Thomas L. Friedman writes: "Uploading responds to a very deep human longing for individuals to participate and make their voices heard."

Blogging answers this longing; "In a blog you can tell the world what you think about any subject." It became so immensely popular that at the time Friedman's book was written, a new blog was created every seven seconds according to *Technorati.com*." Then came "quick blogging" for people in search of constant communication. They use programs such as Twitter to enter two sentences messages into their cell phone and let the network know what they are doing. Another recent social networking tool is Facebook. Thomas Friedman noted that "Thanks to *Facebook.com*, an online social directory, millions of young people now have a platform for telling their own stories." After September 2006, "Facebook" became fairly easily accessible to everyone and, as a result, by mid 2008 it might have contained a collection of data on one hundred million "faces."

The Internet answers people's quest to connect with others. It opens doors to the real world but is also a way to build a digital personality. People find it hard to resist the powerful pull of virtual worlds and virtual identities. They seem to enjoy joining a faceless community at the click of a mouse. Protected by the anonymity offered by the Internet, they succumb to pettiness and asocial instincts. In the best of cases, only civility disappears. The Yahoo finance site of a company that I used to work for has a "message board," which is open to anyone and where nobody ever gives any personal information. It regularly features nasty, vulgar, irrelevant messages posted by contributors known only by an electronic ID. In the worst cases, virtual identities are used to defraud and commit crimes.

There is nothing new in men hiding behind a mask and endorsing several identities, but no social context has ever offered the limitless opportunities of the Internet for good and for bad.

Most people look to others to help them find themselves. They find these others first and foremost in their families. They also find them by joining tribes or groups. Fans are members of tribes, and people sharing religious, political, or ideological creeds belong to groups. These communities provide the eyes that satisfy their need to be acknowledged. These eyes are also the mirrors in which people hope to see themselves. It gives life to their identities.

THE MAKING OF AN IDENTITY

A man's identity is what sets him apart and delineates his difference with the others, but it is also his passport to social relationship. How and why people join tribes and groups is closely connected to how their identities were formed.

Understanding the making of an identity is essential to understanding the making of fans and fanatics.

It has been said that memory and identity are inseparable. The title of this chapter is a citation from Sigmund Freud: "Mankind never lives completely in the present because identity perpetuates the past." More poetically, F. Scott Fitzgerald writes in the last sentence of *The Great Gatsby*: "So we beat on, boats against the current, borne back ceaselessly into the past." In other words, we are a bundle of memories, and they are the sources of our identity and the connectedness to our lineage.

Most men understand intuitively that the histories that they inherited when they were born and the memories they have acquired since then are intimately connected with what they are. They were born with a sex, a race, usually a nationality, sometimes a religion. They observe that knowledge of what has happened to women, black people, and Jews in the past has shaped the way others see women, blacks, and Jews, and how they see themselves.

This does not mean that after it has crystallized, our identity is immutable. Some philosophers have rejected the notion of inherent identity and believe that it can be a construct of the will (Note 2). They theorize that people, groups, or nations can shed the weight of the past and dynamically build an identity. We all have witnessed people shedding or changing features of their identity. Research has shown that an increasing percentage of Hispanics are abandoning church (mostly the Catholic Church) as they become assimilated in the U.S. They feel that what was part of them in the environment of their home country is not essential any more.

Understanding identity formation is helped by using concomitantly a pragmatic and theoretical approach.

When Benjamin, my first grandson, was born in December 2006, so much of what he could become was there before he understood the world around him. He is a white male, was baptized in a Catholic church, and carries an American and a French passport. These are a few of his sources of identity. His life experiences will determine how important each one will be to him. Between now and the end of his adolescence, he will learn to adapt to his environment and to live with others. These will be crucial years in forming his identity. He will observe his parents, learn from his teachers, and imitate his peers.

Erik Erikson has analyzed the importance of this period in the forming of a "healthy" adult. His biographies say that as a young boy he experienced some conflict because of his Jewish faith and his Danish ancestry. This, it is argued, may have caused his interest in identity as a research area. He met Anna Freud, attended the Vienna Psychoanalytic Society, spent his life in the field of human sciences, and was a professor of human development at Harvard. He died in 1994 after having spent most of his life in the U.S. He was an "ego theorist." His contribution to the understanding of man's psychological development is to have recognized the important role the social environment plays. For Erikson, the healthy individual has adjusted to the social and historical circumstances which he or she has faced throughout his or her life.

In his major work, *Childhood and Society,* written in 1950, he introduces the concept that to become a healthy person the individual's ego must successfully progress through a sequence of eight stages from infancy to adulthood. He associates each one with a specific psychological struggle (such as trust vs. mistrust, autonomy vs. doubt or identity vs. role confusion during adolescence). By adolescence, in the fifth stage, between the ages of twelve and eighteen, the ego must deal with the crystallization of identity, with the formation of a sense of self-continuity. This sense of continuity, in other words, being at ease with oneself and harboring an affinity for one's community, is the foundation of ego identity.

In Erikson's works, the term "identity" expresses this mutual relationship. It connotes both a persistent sameness within oneself and a persistent sharing of some kind of essential character with others. A healthy young boy will reconcile his perception of himself and his community's recognition of him. He will need to be recognized not for what he achieves but what he represents. Erikson fathered the concept of "identity crisis," which comes when the sense of sameness and continuity and the belief in one's social role are gone.

How does this apply to Benjamin? By the time he goes to college, he will hopefully have reached a sense of his identity. For example, he will have kept the ties to his French ancestors if they reflect positively on him or have left them dormant because this is not how he wants to be singled out in his community. More relevant to the theme of his book: he most likely will have become a New York Giants fan because his maternal grandfather is a serious fan of the "Big Blue" and inherited his father's identification with the Arsenal soccer team. These teams will be associated with memories of highly emotional moments with his family, and he might be comfortable with these sources of his identity.

He will belong to different communities, the major ones being his family and his peers, friends and schoolmates. Hopefully, he will be at ease with himself and how he is recognized by these groups. If he is a Giant and Arsenal fan, it will be part of his self and part of how others perceive him. He will belong to the world of sport fans. As such, he will have developed strategies to cope with the negative consequences of this fanhood, such as "cutting off reflective failures" in the lingo of social psychologists.

His destiny might also be to go down other paths. Circumstances might be such that Benjamin will have been exposed to a religious, political, or ideological cause during his adolescence. He might have joined friends at a meeting, become enthusiastic about an idea, shared the bond connecting like-minded people. The emotional content of such an event reinforced by the presence of peers will have led him to become an active member of a Church, campaign tirelessly for his congressman, or devote much of his free time to a charitable organization. It will become part of his identity, how he perceives himself, and how others see him. He will be comfortable with, and protective of this source of his identity.

In any case, his social history and the circumstances of his life will have offered him multiple opportunities to shape his identity. He might have rejected what was given to him, but he will have had opportunities to socialize while delineating his differences with others. If during the crucial stages of his identity formation, mostly his adolescence, he acquires the essential building blocks of the identity of a healthy individual, such as trust, he will be able to transcend himself. In other words, he will be able to share with others while preserving his own self.

This is not everyone's destiny. It is a familiar theme, at the beginning of the 21st century, that men encounter problems with traditional sources of identity. Family ties can be loose or non-existent. Among those who have jobs, some feel that it is a source of subordination, that their identity is silenced. The jobless remain alienated, marginalized by society. In all these cases, people are struggling to achieve a sense of recognition, of belonging.

FANS AND FANATICS

When their sources of identity are weak, absent, or do not project a positive image people look to causes or tribes to fill the gap. The community they join or the team they identify with will be determined mostly by their personal history and by circumstances. Family and peers are strong determinants for some, a memorable game or a fortuitous sermon by a charismatic preacher will determine the fate of others.

Most people are born into an affiliation with a sport team, or a religious organization. Young adults are introduced to "their" team by their father. In the Western world, they practice the religion of their parents. When politics is the topic "I have been a Democrat/Republican all my life," reminds one of "I have been a Yankee/Red Sox fan all my life."

A growing number of people make deliberate choices. They are found among those moving into a new city or country who leave behind benchmarks which delineated their specificity. To rebuild an identity they let themselves be attracted by some of the groups or tribes that now surround them.

The fan or the man endorsing a cause become part of a tribe or group that he can call "us." He feels protected against the "others," the supporters of the other teams or the believers in other creeds. His belonging will become part of his identity, and he will develop strategies to cope with any attack against his tribe or group. If an important element of his identity is being a sports fan, he will become fully committed; if it is sharing the doctrine of a political party, he will become intransigent and uncompromising in dealing with the tenets of this doctrine.

Fans and fanatics also share behavioral traits.

When sports fans watch a game, they are taken out of themselves. Most of them thoroughly enjoy the experience and look forward to the next competition; they know that they need to do other things, those that matter in human life and learn to escape the attraction of sports. Some, though, can be excessively enthusiastic. Josef Rudin writes in "*Fanaticism*" that passionate people have a touch of fanatic tendency. They have no reasonable control of their obsession. I know of perplexing stories of fans ignoring milestone family reunions, missing a nephew's baptism or a brother's wedding because "their" team was playing on the same day and time. "Football widows" are quick to recall such gems.

People endorsing a cause are as unable to change their views as sport fans are to abandon their team/athlete. Accepting to see the flaws in their opinions would be as damaging to their ego as playing Judas when their team is in trouble.

It is mostly the object of their involvement which distinguishes fans from fanatics. Professor James V. Schall, who taught for many years at Georgetown University, wrote about things valued "for their own sake." These things are interesting in themselves, are not done out of necessity and follow rules which are mostly arbitrary. Fans are involved in things that exist for their own sake.

This concept can be illustrated by contrasting "sports" and "news" coverage on TV. I was fortunate to hear a lecture by Sean McManus at the time when he was president of both CBS News and CBS Sports. As he pointed out, mistakes in "News" reporting can have serious repercussions; a poor job in reporting a sport event is just that, a poor job; nobody gets hurt.

People can talk about their obstinacy for things that they do for their own sake. When fans are in their real world, not in the "for its own sake" one during sports competitions, they acknowledge their inflexibility and excessiveness. They are not embarrassed to talk about their addiction and can freely admit to being blinded by their passion. They readily proclaim that they are prisoners of their attachment to a team/athlete/sport and more precisely, that they are held captive by a name, a bundle of memories, and a huge investment of emotional energy.

The same men or women will deny being intransigent when the affairs of state are discussed or when the topics are ideologies or religion. This, by the way, explains why dialogues about political or religious issues are never more than the fruitless clash of monologues.

Understanding the making of fans, specifically the anatomy of sports fans, and listening to their stories about catching the virus might help decipher why men stay obstinately attached to political or ideological views

❆ ❆ ❆

NOTE 2

In his book *Once Upon a Country,* Sari Nusseibeh refers to a "theory of identity" as a dynamic function of the will, "whether… of the self or of the nation."

CHAPTER 2

"Why has the relationship that began as a schoolboy crush endured for nearly a quarter of a century...?"
<u>Fever Pitch</u>, **the story of Nick Hornby's obsession with Arsenal, the London soccer team.**

Fans are members of all sorts of "tribes." Some esoteric ones involving only women can be discovered in *Theorizing Fandom, Fans, Subculture and Identity,* a work cited in the Introduction. Slash fans create fanzines, which are collections of fictions based primarily on characters and topics from television series. These fans enjoy their freedom to create and recreate over and over again new lives and adventures for well-known characters. Soap opera fans try to be active participants in the creative process of television series. It is a communal affair, and belonging to a group gives meaning to this activity. Refund fans collect coupons wherever they can find them and were connected through a periodical called "Refunding Makes Cents."

The best known fans are found in the world of leisure activities. Movie actors and actresses, singers, and athletes have devoted followers: young girls who track the whereabouts and wardrobes of movie stars and boys who know every stat of a baseball team. They are members of communities of like-minded people. Belonging to a group comforts and reinforces their identities. Most will be excessive in their behavior. Sports fans, particularly, will exhibit high levels of excitement when they are in their other world. It is the anatomy of this tribe that is at the core of this book.

How does one become a sports fan, a true sports fan? In most cases, people do not pick the object of their attachment; it results from their personal history or from a fortuitous event. The bond with a specific sport/team/athlete becomes a source of identity and, if created during adolescence, is very difficult to break.

In 1980, my family and I moved from France to San Francisco. The eyes of our son Nicholas, who was nine years old at the time, were opened to a new world. He learned another language and discovered American football. The team that entered his life was called the Oakland Raiders, and to this day he has been a Raiders fan. We stayed barely more than one year in the Bay area, but he has never wavered in his commitment. For the longest time, he reacted with exuberance to the club's ups and downs. In that he was not different from other highly committed fans. As the performance of the Raiders was desperately poor in recent years, he has become less emotional and more sentimental. He has stayed true to a memory throughout all these years, against his better judgment.

J.T., a friend of Nick, has followed another path. He picked which English soccer team he was going to support when he was already an adult, and having invested enough energy and built enough memories, his attachment is by now as strong as that of any other Tottenham fan.

Mostly, though, the team puts its brand on the fan, and the major determinants are family, friends, and the places where one has lived.

Books on sports in the U.S. abound in euphoric remembrances of sons being taken to their first ball game by their fathers and how this has resulted in a life-long attachment to a team. Pictures of "the first time I went to see my team play" belong in the family album next to "me and my first dog." In England, a favorite sport fan book is the already mentioned *Fever Pitch,* which takes one through nearly a quarter century of a relationship between the author and the London soccer team of Arsenal. Nick Hornby started to write this book about being a fan in 1991. His father had taken him to an Arsenal game at Highbury in North London in 1968, and "Just this afternoon started the whole thing off, there was no prolonged courtship and I can see that if I had gone to White Hart Lane or Stamford Bridge the same thing would have happened so overwhelming was the experience the first time." (Note: these are the homes of two other London soccer teams.)

The role played by his family and the arbitrariness of the process are the defining features of Hornby's experience. The catalyst of the reaction between him and Arsenal is his father. The team which will become such a central feature of his identity could have been any other soccer team chosen by his father. A similar autobiographical novel could have been written by an American baseball fan. Actually, a movie called *Fever Pitch* combining a hymn to baseball with the familiar elements of a romance was released in April 2005. The script is loosely based on Hornby's book, and the main protagonist is an obsessive Red Sox fan; Highbury or Fenway Park are similar temples for the "fanatici."

Rudy Giuliani, the ex-major of New York, has told the following story many times. Around 1950, the Giulianis lived in Brooklyn, which, as everybody baseball fan knows, was Dodger territory. Rudy's father was rooting for the Yankees. In a character building exercise, he once sent his son

to play in the street dressed in pinstripes. This was a dangerous provocation, even by a child, and young Rudy had to
withstand the threats of the neighborhood gang. He proudly
refused to renounce the attachment to his father's team, and
"I kept telling them: 'I am a Yankee fan, I am gonna stay a
Yankee fan,' it was like being a martyr, 'I'm not going to give
up my religion, you're not gonna change me.'"

The father-son duo at the ball game is the template, but
quite a few women have memories that they love to share.
Once, at a dinner, I sat next to a Norwegian lady, and as
"sports fans" became the topic of our conversation, she
shared the following memory. As a young girl, she went to
an exhibition soccer game where her home town, I think
Bergen, was playing Aston Villa Football Club from the English premiership. The visitors trounced the home boys. She
became in awe of the team that could beat so severely her
local heroes, and to this day is a fan of Aston Villa. Everyone,
man or woman, who has had a similar experience, is happy
to recall it and to indulge in moments of nostalgia.

The teams of people's high school, college, or hometown
are natural candidates for attachment. The fanhood picture,
painted with a broad brush, would show strong connections
with hometowns in Europe and equally strong ones with
high school and college in the U.S.

Sports in educational institutions in Europe never reach
the level of intensity and quality seen in their counterparts
in America even though there are notable exceptions, a la
Oxford-Cambridge. This is particularly striking when very
young people are involved. All Europeans witnessing their
first Little League Baseball or Pop Warner football game are
dumbfounded. The seriousness of the competition, the quality of the coaching and refereeing, the up-to-date equipment,

and the noticeable devotion of the parents elevate a game among children to the level of an institution. This remains true in the U.S through college and results in strong ties with school teams. High school football in Texas and basketball in Indiana are a major part of the identity of people in these states. The identification with college teams can be a lifelong affair, witness the passion of the fans of the Notre Dame Irish or Alabama Crimson Tide. A small but influential group of these college fans devotes time and money to the athletic programs of their Alma Mater. As they obsessively seek the best athletes and coaches for their team, they struggle to stay within the boundaries of the rules of collegiate sports. They fit the profile of the man of Kant, seeker of power and glory.

In Europe, most people do not live too far from where they were born or went to school. The attachment to the hometown or those cities that have played a role in their youth is solid. Rivalries between teams of different towns are deepened by the weight of memories. Anyone who has studied the history of Italy at the time of the Renaissance is familiar with the feuds between and even within cities. They are kept alive, witness the wild folkloric Palio horse race which every year pits the "contrata" (i.e. the neighborhoods) of Siena against each other. The animosity of years past is known to survive on the soccer fields of Florence or Parma, Verona or Vicenza. The teams are the armies defending the honor of the cities. Unfortunately, tifosi in these and other stadiums can also behave like "hooligans." Sport fans in Italy, mainly those found around Ferrari formula one race cars and where soccer is played, are called tifosi, the ones overcome by tifo, i.e typhoid fever. On Sundays, around soccer fields in Italy, it seems that man is not more civilized than at the time of the Medici.

And then there are the young adolescents in neighborhoods across the U.S and Europe who are indulging in whatever game is available to them. For many, this is their only source of pleasure and belonging. They dribble a basketball, swing a baseball bat or kick a soccer ball (in poor areas, often makeshift balls). These sports will be a tie to their community and a feature of their social identity throughout their lives.

Fans attach themselves to memories and facts. To be a fan of the Yankees in 2008 is not an emotional identification with an organization headed by George Steinbrenner, a team led by Derek Jeter or one that played at the "old" Yankee Stadium. It is a deep bond with all things called "Yankee," all the memorable games, the players who became icons, the statistics of each season and, more importantly, a name. Each fan has his own personal relationship with the Yankees or, for that matter, the Red Sox, Raiders, New York Giants or Arsenal. His own ties have been built over time, made of memories, experiences, and knowledge. The fans of a team share the same statistics, the same great moments, and are the safekeepers of its name. Each one, though, has his own stories, which he loves to recall and to tell.

People of all ages in search of an identity may form an emotional attachment to a sport and passionately support whichever team/athlete enhances the image of their nation, race, or religion. Indelible marks, though, are left by events that take place during adolescence. The stories of my son and Nick Hornby attest to this. The life of my grandson might also. While he progresses through the stages of his identity formation, as defined by Erik Erikson, he will encounter events that are more significant than others. The first time a specific team/athlete will enter his life might be such a moment. It will be stored in his memory and become part of him and of how he is perceived by his community. Becoming unfaithful or indifferent to that team/athlete would injure his identity.

Introspective "true" fans know that being a fan is part of their personality. Everything that happens to their team happens to them. It reflects on their self-image and influences their relationship with others. A loss by their team is a personal defeat; it is not an event which happens outside of their lives. Fans use the same thought process to talk about it that they did when trying to justify a C at school: "It's the referee's fault" is another version of "The teacher doesn't like me."

The bond with a team/sport is a feature of the true fan's social persona. People around him know that he is a fan and he is treated as a peer by all those who share his passion. They challenge his knowledge, engage him in bets, or mock him when his team loses. The "out-group" looks at him with condescension. As for his family, he makes their choice of a Christmas gift easy; they just buy him one more piece of clothing or memorabilia with the logo of his team.

Can a fan escape what fate has put in his path? Can he abandon "his" team and identify with a rival one? It is well documented that people adopting a new creed in the political, social, or religious sphere become excessive in their new commitment and in their criticism of the one they have abandoned. They want to be seen as uncompromising believers in their new cause. Sports fans can repudiate what they have worshiped or more simply silence their fanhood. In either case, even if they can ignore their memories, they will not be able to erase them.

MEMORIES

In the early 50's, on most Sundays during soccer season, my father would drive with my mother and me to various towns in the east of France. He was an inspector for the League of French Soccer Referees and supervised the performance of the referee at some designated game. There was no partisanship involvement by my father. Being the referee of referees is like being neutral in a neutral country. There was even less excitement for my mother and me.

We would watch some of the games, stay in a warm place on cold winter afternoons, or visit the town. I remember a few places: Ornans, many years later I saw a painting by Gustave Courbet at the Musee d'Orsay featuring the cemetery I had passed by many times; Pontarlier, we used to make a detour through nearby Switzerland to buy milk chocolate and on the way out of town see the fort where Toussaint l'Ouverture, who led the revolt against the French in Haiti in the early 1800's had been imprisoned.

Soccer entered my life in a quiet way during that time. No bursts of enthusiasm, just a cool appreciation of a game that was a proud feature of my father's life. Anyway, in those days, in France, it was not proper for a teenager aspiring to belong to the bourgeoisie of his home town to be too involved in soccer. This was not part of the curriculum of the sons of doctors, lawyers or university professors, and even less so of their daughters. Soccer did provide socially acceptable excitement every four years during the World Cup. For a few weeks, everybody became a supporter of the national team. I would listen intently on the radio to the games played by the French team and still have sweet memories of Just Fontaine scoring goal after goal in Sweden in 1958. Later, in my twenties, I would share the excitement of my friends in front of a TV set.

Soccer was never a passionate affair, no love at first sight, but it became a constant companion. It is part of my identity—this has not been changed by half a lifetime spent in the US.

CHAPTER 3

"War minus the shooting."

George Orwell.

How sport became what it is today is a story worth telling, and as usual when dealing with features of Western societies, a good starting point is Greece.

Classical Greek culture was characterized by an agonistic spirit, a love of competing and of winning. Athletic contests were all about winning, not about participating. This was true of the Olympic Games, which became the main sports events after the eighth century BC. When Pierre de Coubertin revived them on an international scale in 1896, his motto, "The most important thing is not winning but taking part," was well-adapted to the gentlemen amateurs of that time but had little to do with the Greek origin of the games.

Greece's popular competitions featured combats whose ultimate purpose was training for warfare in the form of wrestling, boxing, and "pankration" (a combination of boxing and modern professional wrestling with simple rules: no biting or eye gouging and victory secured through KO, surrendering, or death). Spectators were as partisan and excitable as modern fans. Lovers of trivia know that athletes initially competed naked; they started using loincloths by the early fifth century BC. Their nudity, the story goes, was a way for the Greek citizens to distinguish themselves from clothed barbarians and slaves. Trivia lovers also know that women, except for priestesses, were prohibited from watching the contests, and it was not until the first century BC that they had their own competitions.

In Rome, the most popular games were chariot races and gladiatorial combats. The races held in circuses attracted huge crowds. The Circus Maximus is said to have accommodated up to 250,000 people. Rival factions were distinguished by the color of their tunics – the Whites and the Reds initially and the Blues and the Greens by the mid second century. Just like the Greeks before them and today's fans, supporters were identifying with their favorite team. Most books on the history of sport quote the Roman author Pliny the Younger: "It is the racing colors that they really support and care about" and how he derides the popularity of a "worthless shirt." Romans also enjoyed watching violent games staged in amphitheaters. The best known was the Coloseum inaugurated by Titus in 80 AD. The spectacles were eagerly awaited even though the actors were considered lowlifes. The Circus Maximus and the Coloseum were popular places in Rome and offered opportunities to confront the Emperor. Games were a safety valve for dissatisfaction. In the 21st century, stadiums during sport events are still a place where the opposition can, with a minimal risk of reprisal, express its feelings about the power in place.

Most traditional and popular games were banned by the first Christian Emperors. In the 5th century, Theodosius II ordered the destruction of pagan temples, including the one at Olympia. The site was further damaged by the barbarians who overran the Roman Empire. It can be visited today, and while looking at the excavated gymnasium, the stadium or the palaestra with its re-erected columns, one can form a picture of the athletes competing and almost hear the crowd. Chariot racing survived for a few more centuries in the eastern part of the Empire, and spectators would continue to exhibit little control over their partisanship.

The social context for games changed with the end of the Empire and the emergence of Christianity. During the Middle Ages and the Renaissance, the life of communities was centered on churches, cathedrals, and markets, not amphitheaters and circuses. Sports become more class specific and attracted smaller crowds. Archery competitions were popular in continental Europe; spectators came at annual events also to enjoy other forms of entertainment. Tournaments were opportunities for crowd gathering, and movie buffs know that the scenes in *Ivanhoe* are subdued compared to the wild race in *Ben Hur.*

Allen Guttmann writes in *Sport Spectators* that the medieval ballgame which eventually evolved into soccer, rugby, and football is the folk sport about which we are the best informed. Up until the second half of the 19th century, it knew no rules constraining the crowd's excitement, no boundaries and limits to the size of the field of play, spectators and players commingled, all actors in wild chases across countryside and village streets. It must have been like Ashbourne Royal Shrovetide Football, a game which is now played every year on Shrove Tuesday and Ash Wednesday in Ashbourne, Derbyshire, England. Two teams, numbering in the hundreds, represent those born on the northern or southern side of the River Henmore. The playing field is three miles long, two miles wide, and has the town of Ashbourne in the middle. The crowd of players ebbs and flows most of the day up to the time one of them scores a goal by striking a mill wheel three times with the ball. This folkloric tradition is an instructive yearly reenactment of how ball games were once played.

While the Greeks applauded the exploits of individual athletes some forms of team sports were practiced elsewhere.

In its history of soccer, the FIFA, soccer's governing body, refers to a Mesoamerican ballgame played several centuries BC. Courts can still be seen in Maya temples, and the "goals" attached to the walls always intrigue today's visitors.

There is little disagreement in the academic world that modern sports began in England. Norbert Elias, the Swiss sociologist, dates their origin to the second half of the 18th century when the parliamentary regime in England had its beginnings. The fundamental feature of such a system which was more fully implemented after the middle of the 19th century is that those who are not elected accept to withdraw peacefully. We know that since then this rule has not always been respected, but the basic principle of not using violence to contest the result of an election remains the key to democratic regimes. Elias in *Quest for Excitement*, a book that he co-authored with Eric Dunning in 1986, argues that this peaceful acknowledgement of the results of elections opened the door to modern sports. Competitive sport as we know it today became possible when rules were agreed upon by everyone, spectators were separated from players, contests took place in a specific space, and national federations came into being.

English colleges gave the impetus to the codification of what would become soccer and rugby. During the autumn of 1863, representatives of English public schools met and attempted to unify the different rules that were used in playing the game called soccer. Some, from the Rugby school, favored allowing the use of hands. Others preferred to have the ball dribbled not carried. The latter created the Football Association on October 26. Eighteen clubs agreed to respect fourteen laws, which prescribed among others the size of the playing field: "the length of the ground shall be 200 yards, the maximum breadth shall be 100 yards," when a player would be offside and that "neither tripping nor hacking shall be allowed." Those in favor of playing "rugby" created their own Rugby Football Union in 1871. The immediate consequence of this process was to make the playing field even and create conditions for fair competition. This was a major shift from free-for-all games and allowed the development of contests at a time when the secretary of the Richmond Club would write: "various clubs play to rules which differ from others which makes the game difficult to play."

American football is derived from Rugby, whose rules were progressively changed after 1880. Many innovations were the brainchildren of Walter Camp. Born in New Haven in 1859, he attended Yale where he played American football. The history books say that he edited every American Football Rulebook until his death in 1925. As the intensity on the field was leading to widespread violence, rules were introduced at the beginning of the 20th Century to make the game less dangerous. Among the changes was the legalization of the forward pass. A moment in history: in 1879, a boarding school for American Indians was established in Carlisle, Pennsylvania; a few years later, the students took up American Football. Coached by "Pop" Warner, a name familiar to young football lovers, they developed innovative trick plays. In 1907, the "Indians" were the first team to regularly throw the ball deeply downfield.

The basic rules of soccer as we know them today had more or less been agreed upon by the end of the 19th century but have since then been constantly adapted or modified. For instance, those dealing with the number of players that can be substituted, the nature of the physical contact between a field player and the opponent's goalie or the definition of offside have been changed over time. The history of these changes is interesting in itself because it shows the influence of certain national federations. The English have always tried to keep the game virile and aggressive, while the Americans have been looking to make it into a "show" with more goals being scored; the NASL even suggested thirty second TV time-outs in 1975.

There is no single definition of "sport," but scholars generally agree that physical activity needs to be involved and that conditions allowing for "fair" competitions are to be met. Fair, in this context, means that competitors are on an equal footing, the result of one competition comparable to that of others played under similar conditions.

This agreement on rules, which is an essential feature of the perennity of a sport, does not imply that they are immutable. How they are set requires digging in the archives of each sport. The first codified ones for soccer were based on what made the game pleasurable, challenging, and not too risky to play. These initial rules had little connection to "natural laws" and therefore were changed over time to reflect the desires of competitors and spectators and to adapt to different social environments. This is why E. Hemingway derided sports based on abstract concepts as "merely games," claiming that something is really at stake only in mountaineering, bullfighting, and motor racing. In most cases, new rules aim at making competitions less dangerous and more spectacular, i.e. with more goals/points being scored. Some answer the need to simplify their management; the introduction of tiebreakers has considerably facilitated the planning of tennis tournaments! Others reflect changes in technology and in man's physical abilities; golf courses need to be kept challenging for players who are hitting longer shots. New sports or forms of competitions are created to offer different challenges.

Since the beginning of the twentieth century, the expansion of sports and sport fandom in the world has been almost uninterrupted. The Olympic Games are a useful proxy of sports in general, and their statistics tell the story even though many highly popular spectator sports are not represented. In the first modern Olympic Games in Athens, in 1896, thirteen countries competed in nine sports. The very same Athens in 2004 saw more than eleven thousand athletes representing 202 countries compete in 296 events of twenty-eight sports! The world of sport fandom followed a parallel growth.

The initial cause of the success of this human activity is the growth of urbanization. The bulk of the working class, which was mostly involved in agriculture, moved to the industrial sector and then to the service industries; people left the countryside to relocate in cities. This brought a greater need for physical and outdoor activities and gave people more free time. It is difficult for people involved in agriculture to take regular days off, but starting at the end of the 19th century, workers in England had free Saturday afternoons. More people in cities with more leisure time created a market for spectator sports as attested to by regular sport sections appearing in daily newspapers by the late 19th century. At a time when urbanization had loosened the social fabric, sports offered new opportunities for social interaction and became a growing business. This was true for most Western countries even though there were differences in how social classes adopted sports as participants or spectators. The "gentry" in England, used to country clubs, adopted them fairly naturally while the French aristocracy snubbed them for a long time.

Among other developments which account for the increasing importance of sport in people's life from the 19th century on is the role played by the expansion of colonial empires and world trade. Africans, Asians, and South Americans were introduced to the pleasures of Western sports by the French and even more so by the British. They became worthy competitors of the Europeans. This is still largely true for the sports that England brought to the Commonwealth countries such as rugby. Some students were even more gifted than the teachers. British sailors introduced soccer to Brazil in the second half of the 19th century (another theory is that the first soccer ball was brought to Brazil in 1894 by Charles Miller, the son of a Scottish banker), and the Brazilian national team is one of the best in the world today.

As sports joined the ranks of acceptable social activities, they became again what they were in the Middle Ages, the people's game, an important part of proletarian leisure, a means of preserving the identity of the working class.

In England at the end of the 19th century, the public schools codified soccer and rugby, and the churches created teams. They understood that these games would help develop Christian qualities of fair play and strong character and were at the origin of many clubs still present in the Premier Soccer League.

In the U.S complicity between sport and religion has existed since the 19th century. The American sport creed of individual achievement through competition did fit well with the Protestant ethic, the winners seen as God's chosen people. This has been thoroughly researched by Robert J. Higgs in his book *God in the Stadium, Sports and Religion in America.* He calls the embracing of athletic ability by Christians a form of witnessing, brings to light the inordinate influence of the military academy on American sport, and theorizes that the reverence paid to sport in the U.S. can be explained as a perpetuation of knighthood. The contests of knights are kept alive by the alliance between muscular Christianity, which endorses competition and has a sense of entertainment, and the military with its virtues of obedience and discipline and institutionalized games whose goals are to champion manliness and the art of power.

Religion is never far from the fields of play in America. This is particularly visible in college organizations and is demonstrated by college football coaches expressing publicly their religious affiliations in leading their teams in prayer.

The relationship between sport and religion exists at other levels. Sport has often been referred to as a modern religion (Note 3). The October 2007 magazine of a parish in York, England related the following story. In 1983, the principal of the College of the Resurrection, Mirfield in the West Riding of Yorkshire, wrote a book on prayer in which he compared playing games with prayer, especially liturgical prayer:

> "Games need a set of rules to which the players conform and our services have rules about what is done. Games need the wholehearted commitment of the players and Christian worship needs the dedication of every member of the congregation. A good game rouses the emotions and whatever the result leaves the players with a sense of well-being and satisfaction and a Church service can produce an uplifting religious experience."

The principal could have added other similarities. Sports and religion test the ability of humans to control their body and emotions, athletes and ascetics learn to overcome pain, etc...

A similar piece could be written about the experiences of the Church goers and the sport fans. Karl Marx made provocative statements about sport and religion and called both "opium of the people." Is sport a religion for its fans?

The answer could be a lighthearted one: it seems that attendance at church services is negatively impacted by games played by children on Sunday morning. It is difficult to be both a soccer mom and a church mom.

On a more serious note, church services and sports competitions share a long list of features. They are forums for communion. In both cases, human beings ritualize by performing acts in a repetitive manner. For religious believers there is comfort in saying the same words and making the same signs in repetitive cycles, in doing this in unison with others whatever language they speak. Similarly, the life of sports fans is rich in rituals. Between the middle of August and the end of January, American football fans perform certain acts in the same way every Sunday afternoon and have a ritual on some Monday nights. They find comfort in a routine with others in a stadium or alone in front of a TV.

The faithful and the fans can experience beauty and harmony. They can be exalted by hymns and chants. They can attain a different reality. Sitting in a place of worship or in a stadium offers a reprieve from ordinary reality and helps humans endure the vicissitudes of life. Religion and sports are two activities which satisfy the human need for transcendence.

The list of similarities in form and function is rich and convincing but only to a point. Humans have a thirst for understanding and giving an ultimate meaning to their lives. Organized religions offer their followers a road to "being sure about things." They have faith, a way to a truth. Sport gives order but not meaning. It has no Story to tell, no Good News, just stories and nostalgia, no eschatology, and it does not offer a transforming experience. Calling it a religion for its fans would be elevating it to a level of human experience where it does not belong.

Not unexpectedly, the principal of the College of the Resurrection concluded his comparison by reminding his parishioners that,

"Christian worship is much more than a game, it is about the most profound activity in which we can be involved, the worship of Almighty God, the creator of everything."

At the beginning of the 21st century, sports are ubiquitous in the Western world. Radio, television, newspapers report on results, business deals of clubs, transactions involving athletes or even on their private lives; some papers, radio and TV stations, and numerous "pages" on the internet are devoted solely to sport. Business, religion, and politics receive similar exposure, but sport is the dominant form of popular culture, and it occupies an increasingly large space in the realm of human activities. It plays an important social role in offering to its fans numerous opportunities to join a community and gain an identity. They can become members of different tribes, the fans of their high school, college or home town teams as well as the larger one of supporters of the athletes representing their nation.

ABOUT THE TRIBES OF SPORTS FANS

Spectators exhibiting fanatical traits have been present ever since games have been played. Men, and also women, love competitions and are attracted by physical feats. They seem to endorse instinctively one of the competitors even if no personal gain is at stake. Ardent supporters were present during games in Greece, and excessive manifestations of enthusiasm were also expected of Roman spectators. Uncontrolled behavior by people who had yet to go through a "civilizing process" is not surprising. That it is still exhibited by modern fans is testimony to the power of passions.

The largest tribes of fans are associated with sports supervised by federations/leagues. These recognized bodies set the rules and organize the competitions. They also play a role in balancing the interests of the actors involved, players, owners, spectators as well as cities and states.

The communities of sports fans are dominated by "alpha" males who cherish communing with peers during sports events be it at a bar, in a stadium, or at home. A fair number of women can be seen commingling with them, but despite their enthusiasm and beer drinking ability, they are no counterweight to the maleness of these tribes. There is no worse shame for men than to have a woman win one of the office pools run during the football or basketball season in the U.S. My daughter, Alexandra, the only woman in a college basketball "March Madness" pool, won in 2005 and again in 2006. Some of the men in the pool complained that this was sheer luck (which it certainly was) and in the face of such unfairness conveniently forgot to pay up. Actually, women winning the pool in March seems to be a fairly common occurrence.

Men consider sport their domain. In an age where the roles played by men and women are no longer clearly delineated, it is an area where they claim superiority over women. News coverage overwhelmingly favors events in which men are competing, and this despite a surge in the number of female fans. A study done in the U.S. by Scarborough Sports Marketing shows that the percentage of women eighteen and older who are very or somewhat avid sports fans has gone from 28% in 1998 to 58% in November 2002. Despite this evolution in the composition of its fandom, sport remains an activity where some males go to reinforce their sense of identity.

Fans express their national pride through sports, and this is particularly true of Europeans. They know well how much the image of nations is reflected by its athletes and teams.

Sports competitions have long been used as proxy for war. Competing against the oppressor is a chance of repairing a damaged national identity whenever a country is under the yoke of another. The Czechs derived considerable pride from the victories of their hockey team over the Russians at the time when Czechoslovakia was behind the Iron Curtain. Life in England taught me that, in soccer, when Germany is called the archrival, it has as much to do with the Second World War as with the hard fought battles between the two teams. The same holds true when Holland plays Germany and has the possibility of a belated revenge against an ex-oppressor.

Americans have fewer opportunities to be involved in international competitions. Thanks to its size, the U.S. is self-sufficient for high level competitions, and the most popular sports are indigenous. Football and the national pastime steeped in nostalgia, baseball, have been, for most of their history, specific to the U.S. NASCAR is hugely popular, while the rest of the world from Finland to Brazil is passionate about Formula 1 racing. The U.S. mostly witnesses the excesses of other nations in celebrating sport victories or mourning defeats, except for a few cases when it gets caught in a bout of exuberance—the victory of its hockey team at the Olympic Games in Lake Placid in 1980 is one example.

Victories in international sport competitions have a positive impact on the identity of fans and that of their countrymen, particularly in countries which have few other opportunities to be patriotic. It had been claimed that a victory by the Ivory Coast soccer team at the 2006 African Nations Cup would improve the chances of a reconciliation between the so-called rebels and the government in that country (neither victory nor reconciliation happened). It must be remembered that many governments are more than happy to use sports to pacify their citizens by giving them something to cheer about and that, as Decimus Junius

Juvenal wrote about two thousand years ago, "The people... long eagerly for just two things, bread and circuses (panem et circenses)."

Even though it cannot be disputed that sport allows fans to affirm their national identity, the general public (and the media) are often confused between the apparent manifestation of national pride and the mere opportunity to express wild enthusiasm. Shortly after France's victory over Brazil in a quarter final of the 2006 soccer world cup, my wife and I walked up the Champs Elysees in Paris. Swarms of young people were surging out of the subway station on the Rond Point. The closer we were getting to the Arc de Triomphe, the denser the crowd became, and the side streets were already blocked by the police ready to control groups which would probably need disciplining later in the night. People were singing and dancing in the orange light of high held flares as if following ancient rites. There seemed to be no barrier between all these "fans"; everybody was part of a big tribe, excited and delighted. The event would be reported as a massive demonstration of national pride. We experienced it as an opportunity for men and women, mainly young ones from the Paris suburbs, to be excessive. They seized the moment to join others, to be free to be enthusiastic. After France lost against Italy in the final, I was sad, not because I am French, but because I felt the irrevocability of defeat and was deprived of the great pleasure of calling my children and friends, rejoicing with them and having memories I could cherish.

Sport teams or athletes can be the flag bearers of a race, religion, or local community. In soccer, when Barcelona meets Real Madrid, it is Catalonia against Spain. In years past, when Spartak Prague played Dynamo Moscow, its supporters would seek a small measure of revenge against the KGB.

When, in Scotland, Glasgow Celtic beats Glasgow Rangers, Northern Ireland Catholics celebrate. This last example is the favorite case study used by anyone interested in soccer as a support for identities. In *"Fanatics!"* Joseph Bradley writes:

> "...the vast majority of Catholics in Scotland originate from Ireland and a strong bond exists between many of those Catholics and the Celtic Football club. ...for the Catholic/Irish community, Celtic provides the social setting through which that community's sense of its own identity is sustained, in and through a set of symbolic processes and representations."

In a similar fashion, people in the U.S. commune with their college or local high school teams. In some areas of the country, the identification is very strong. There is the little known story of the passion that wrestling is capable of inspiring in the high schools of Iowa (Note 4); lives revolve around matches and practices of young wrestlers who rarely achieve fame outside of their state. There is the much better known world of high school football in Texas. The saga of a highly successful team, the Odessa Permian Panthers, has been told by H.G Bissinger who, in 1988, left his job as a newspaper editor for the Philadelphia Inquirer and moved to Odessa. For four months he followed every move of the members of the team and in 1990 wrote "Friday Night Lights," which became a bestseller and later a movie and a television series. The book describes how sports give values to towns in West Texas in particular and on their effect on American life in general. It shows the identity of a town entwined with that of its high school football team and also gives a first hand account of what sports mean for high school seniors, the fairytale life and the dramas during one year in their life, a single season to be a prince, a moment to lose it all. In a captivating piece, Bissinger relates the drama of Boobie, his dreams shattered by a knee injury early in his senior season:

> "'I won't be able to play college football, man. It's real important. It's all I ever wanted to do. All I wanted to do,' he whispered again."

The book is about the loneliness of the coach, rendered more cruel after each defeat, about the former Permian Panther stars, some of them endlessly reliving their moments of glory, and about young adults unprepared for life after leaving this other reality of High School Football. The first part of the "Epilogue" recounts the dramatic fall from grace of the two stars of the Carter Cowboys, the 1988 state champions. They had been courted by recruiters, who shamelessly bribed them and made the boldest promises. In their own words, "We was on top of the world," but what gave them a real kick was armed robbery, the first one on May 19,1989, and six more in the space of one month until they were arrested. One was sentenced to twenty years in prison and the other to sixteen. As the prosecutor said:

> "You look at how we treat them in high school and how we treat them in college and everyone asks why they act like children, how would you expect them to act any other way?"

Bissinger's work is above all about a community investing its identity in a team. In the words of a former president of the Permian Booster Club:

> "When somebody talks about West Texas they talk about football. There is nothing to replace it. It's an integral part

of what made the community strong. You take it away and it's almost like you strip the identity of the people."

High school football was at the core of life in Odessa, the way the community had chosen to express itself. Odessa and West Texas, with their men from the oil fields "who made it with muscle, endurance and self sacrifice, the same values that made the boys great on the football field," might be microcosms but are beautiful and tragic examples of what sport can mean to a community.

ℜ ℜ ℜ

NOTE 3

What is meant by "religion" needs to be clarified. In the western world, which is the one we are concerned with in this book, most people have an implicit understanding. To them, religion refers to the set of practices and beliefs found mostly in the monotheist communities called Christian Churches, Judaism, and Islam. The following reflections are based on this understanding of the word.

NOTE 4

The close up portraits of two senior wrestlers are the centerpiece of a book by Mark Kreidler titled *Four Days to Glory, Wrestling With the Soul of the American Heartland.*

CHAPTER 4

*"David Beckham has been catapulted from
the muddy ranks of football players into the
financial stratosphere of show business."*
<u>The Times on line</u>, **January 12, 2007.**

In 1975, Pele, the world-renowned Brazilian soccer player, signed with the New York Cosmos, the best known club from the now defunct NASL. At the beginning of 2007, the English star David Beckham was transferred to the Los Angeles Galaxy, who competes in MLS (note 5). In both cases, the owners of the American clubs were hoping to generate excitement for the world's most popular professional sport, which has yet to gain much ground in the U.S. In both cases, also, the players were on the last leg of brilliant careers. Pele had worn for the last time the green and gold jersey of the Brazilian national team during a friendly game at Maracana against Yugoslavia in 1971, and he scored the last goal of his career during the final game of his three year contract with the American team. As for Beckham, the jury was still out at the start of his American campaign. He had remained a member of the English national squad even though he had often been on the bench during his last season with his former club, Real Madrid. The Cosmos were ahead of their time in being a global brand and no stranger to marketing coups. The Galaxy broke the self-imposed conservatism of their league and indulged in an extravaganza, which might jolt the MLS.

The difference between the two deals is that Pele was to receive $7 million for three years while Beckham's five year package has been reported to be worth more than $200 million. The amounts touted by his agent depend largely on the power of his fame to increase attendance and sales of merchandise, but taken at face value, and even adjusting for inflation, the two packages could be in a ratio close to one to five on a yearly basis. The price of doing business in soccer has increased dramatically, or seen from another angle, a lot more disposable income is spent on soccer at the beginning of the 21st century. Beckham is not expected so much to be an efficient play maker as to be the major attraction of an entertainment package.

SPORT AS ENTERTAINMENT

The expression "sports entertainment" has been around since the 1980's, popularized by the WWF, the World Wrestling Federation, and it can define any scripted sport event. The Harlem Globe Trotters are very gifted basketball players using their skills to entertain, not to compete. Sport as entertainment is another concept. It implies that games involving professional teams are more than mere confrontations on the field of play. They are opportunities for spectators to become consumers of products offered by the club.

Entertainment is wrapped around baseball games in the U.S. Major league and even more so minor league clubs are building on a tradition of family entertainment. They run an endless list of promotions, hand out club T-shirts, organize the signing of autographs by players, and keep the cheers going with fireworks. They offer the comfort of corporate suites, and serious fans can buy their way to rubbing elbows with the stars of the team. Parents can spoil their children with merchandise sporting the name of their favorite player. There are pregame shows. Young boys and girls will be invited to play T ball on the field before the "big" game. And much more. Baseball parks are run like amusement parks.

This is true for other sports. In basketball arenas, there is no "time out" for the spectator. He is constantly entertained with pyrotechnics, cheerleaders, and overuse of the PA system. Sport aficionados can find this overwhelming. Too much sound and a circus atmosphere are distracting and unnecessary when the real drama is the game. My neighbor in the stands at a track meet in New York in June 2007 complained that the loud music and constant commentaries by a quasi D.J pacing around the track was creating a "sensory overload." Who would have thought that even track and field would feel pressured to enter the world of entertainment? All this is designed to attract men and women, young and old, to a stadium and entice them to spend money.

There were elements of show business in sports in the U.S at the time Pele joined the Cosmos, but since then, most professional teams have learned to compete for a share of the revenues of the entertainment industry. David Beckham has great name recognition, an attractive image and a famous pop star wife. American soccer fans will want to see him work his magic, but more importantly, he will generate business for the club and for himself. In a different world, management consultants and legal firms parade ex-stars of the Washington political scene in front of their clients. They are not expected to solve problems, but their presence is flattering for clients, and this way of doing business works. The arrival of the Beckhams in the U.S in July 2007 was a media extravaganza. Victoria's self-indulgent T.V show might have been short- lived, but before David even played his first game, his new MLS team collected enough revenue through additional future gate receipts, sales of licensed products, sponsorship, etc… to cover his salary for his first two seasons.

It has been obvious for a long time that professional sports had features of a successful business proposition. Pete Rozelle understood this. In *America's Game,* Michael MacCambridge relates how after Rozelle's election as commissioner in 1960, his public relations savvy and smart decisions made the NFL into a business success. More recently investors, mostly American, have estimated that soccer clubs in England can make for attractive investments. In the spring of 2005, Malcolm Glazer, who regularly appeared on Forbes' list of the 400 richest Americans and was already owner of the pro football Tampa Bay Buccaneers, gained control of Manchester United. Two years later, in early 2007, Tom Hicks and George Gillett took over the Liverpool F.C. George Gillett has a long history of investing in sports, specifically in the Montreal Canadiens hockey team. Tom Hicks, after leaving the buy-out firm of Hicks, Muse, and Associates in 2004, transferred his energy to managing his investments in two Dallas professional sport teams, the Rangers and the Stars.

The Manchester United and Liverpool business models are based on the acknowledgment that professional teams generate more revenues than gate receipts alone. The sale of television rights has been for many years a major source of income. Private boxes and food sales during games contribute to the bottom line. This has become such a visible feature of sports events that Michel Platini, the former soccer star who became president of the Union of European Football Associations, said in a tone reflecting his exasperation, "The purpose of sport is not to sell hot-dogs at half-time." Aggressive marketing of the logo of soccer and baseball clubs follows the worldwide spread of their fame. Sales of jerseys, caps, and other paraphernalia carry high margins. The decisions to invest in European soccer teams are based on two other justifications: real estate is often part of the assets that are purchased and consequently a factor in the expected financial return and ownership of a sport club is an extraordinary ego booster for self-made billionaires.

The Beckham transaction is also another demonstration that trading athletes knows no borders. Russians on the ice, Japanese around the baseball diamonds, and Europeans on the basketball courts are common sights in the U.S. Soccer players are freely traded inside of the European Union. The globalization of sport was visible during the 2006 Soccer World Cup. Most national teams were led by players from squads of a handful of European club teams. The antics of a young man playing for Portugal convinced the referee to red card a forward from the English team while both were partners at Manchester United during the regular season.

The access to a worldwide pool of athletes and more money to offer to the best has leveled the field of competitors. In most major professional sports, several teams are at parity "on paper" during any given season. As anything can happen and anyone can win on any day, the identification of spectators is reinforced. Sport as entertainment means performance. People watching a competition don't search for aesthetics and beauty, they want efficiency, and they want to be on the winning side. Who cares how the goal was scored as long as it wins the game? This "must win" in a context of constant uncertainty over the performance of a team or athlete dramatically increases the tension during certain competitions. It makes for exciting shows and enhances the entertaining side of professional sport.

The need to give every team in their league a chance to be competitive has been understood for some time now by the commissioners of the major U.S professional organizations. Parity preserves the economic value of franchises and the interest for the game. The NFL and NBA hold yearly drafts meant to handicap the best and favor the worst of the preceding season.

Fans are encouraged when their team recruits talented players, but they know that victories are the result of good fortune and "guts" as much as skill. Lucky breaks bring smiles, and great memories are built when their athlete or team have found in themselves the will to win.

Money can buy talent, superior training, and coaching, but not spirit. In September 2007, during the very last days of the season, the Philadelphia Phillies overtook the New York Mets, a team loaded with talent that had been dominant throughout the year and won the baseball National League East title. This prompted Pat Gillick, their general manager to say.

"Talent is important but what is more important is mental toughness, character, passion and the desire to win."

A few weeks later, the French rugby team beat New Zealand in a quarter final of the Rugby World Cup. The All Blacks were clearly the better team and would win any best of three series. But on that day, they could not dispose of an adversary who, as the French press wrote, had the heart, will, and guts to win. Neither the Phillies nor the French rugby team went any further on their path to title and glory. Maybe they ran out of mental resources or luck, or their success had merely resulted from the mathematics of random phenomena. They ended up robbing their fans of their dreams, but their spirited performance had given them great joy and immense excitement.

The last days of the 2008 regular baseball season were déjà vu for the Phillies but this time momentum carried them all the way to the World Series title. The interviews on the field, after the last out, were all on the same theme,

"Thank you to the fans; wouldn't have done it without them."

A SCHOOL FOR MORAL VALUES?

Despite the changing context in which professional sports operate, sport in general is still viewed as a school for moral values and mental discipline. It is said to inculcate behavior patterns which are beneficial to society. Usually cited are: athletes show pride in their heritage, their schools, and their country; they learn that improvement comes through rigorous practice and acceptance of pain; they put the performance of their team above their own success, foster team spirit, and know how to trust and follow leaders; they accept that losing is part of playing. Most people who have been involved with sports when they were young will claim that this experience has helped them develop moral virtues and mental strength.

Politicians, business executives, and entertainers are usually keen to talk about what sport means to them. Typically, they became involved at a young age, pushed by their father, and competing with siblings. They remember that they were hooked by the thrill of competing. With this competitive spirit goes the importance of winning, and they will affirm sententiously that "people who quit never win" or "know how to lose to know how to win." Sport taught them perseverance and hard work, and they believe that it always gives one a chance to come back. They give accolades to team spirit, belonging to a group, and winning as a team. They always come back to the love of competing, which is not surprising for people who are highly successful in their domain.

Donald Trump said:

"I am not sure if I was a competitive person who played sports or became more competitive because of sports …." (Note 6)

These features of sport, which happen to be appreciated by American society, can have, unfortunately, a negative side. The drive for performance can lead to aggressivity. The need for discipline opens the door to authoritarianism. Most coaches require blind obedience, and some, when they are successful, are idolized for their tyrannical behavior. Herb Brooks, the coach of the U.S Olympic hockey team, which performed the so-called "Miracle on Ice" victory over the Soviet Union at the 1980 Lake Placid Olympics, is a telling example of such an icon. He did not want to be the friend of his players as he forcefully broke down their college hockey affiliations to recast them into Team U.S.A. Educators will say that learning blind obedience is appropriate for "war games" and military discipline and is not what young people should practice after they graduate, but it is difficult to argue with success. The agonistic spirit which already drove the ancient Greeks can lead people to forget about moral values, but this can also be said about business and politics.

The drive to win should not deter athletes from the need to "play fair." They know that if performance is to be measured and comparisons over time made possible, they must compete on a "level playing field." They must respect the rules, even if these are mostly abstract and without natural foundation. This is the essence of institutionalized sports, just as fair voting is essential to the democratic process. It can be said that sport competitions inculcate good principles in citizens of democratic countries. Unfortunately, playing fair has become less and less a feature of professional sports, the activities with which fandom is mostly associated. Before elaborating on this statement, it is worthwhile to observe a particular tribe of the world of sports.

Cordoned off from professionalism and belonging in the world of amateur sports are the young athletes and their parents involved in baseball, football, soccer, hockey, basketball, and other games played in and around schools and particularly high schools in the U.S. On the sidelines of any of these team games one can see and hear parents who care mostly about their child's performance and are biased towards the referee. They may be full of good intentions, but when the games start, they seem only to have their self-interest at heart. This is not a recent phenomenon. Parents have always used their children as proxies for what they themselves would have liked to achieve, and this holds true for other human activities besides sport. What is new is that since the early 90's the behavior of some parents has changed for the worse. They are no longer only highly motivated fans of their children, they have become real fanatics, aggressive towards opponents, referees and more and more, coaches.

This is another manifestation of the impact of money on the behavior of those associated with sport. As the cost of college education is inexorably climbing and competition for admission becoming ever tighter, parents have been placing their bets on the edge that athletic abilities can give to their children's college and scholarship applications. They sacrifice their free time to coach, drive, and support the budding athlete and make heavy emotional and financial investments in their children's athletic development. In this context, it is understandable if not excusable that obstacles on the road to success, in the highly emotionally charged atmosphere of sports events, will provoke irrational behavior. Parents, mostly fathers, will react violently if their child is "benched" or not selected for the A team, or when faced with any action that potentially damages the young athlete's resume. In June

2005, the New York Times reported that in Hamden, Connecticut:

> "M. P. upset that his daughter, M., had been suspended for missing a softball game to attend a prom, clubbed coach J.C. in the back of the head with an aluminum bat."

The article contained other examples of similar behavior at high school football and hockey games.

A SCHIZOPHRENIC WORLD

Athletes are rewarded based on how successfully they perform. This statement has been true throughout the history of sport, but the implications for professionals have become more dramatic. The pot of gold is so big, the cost of failure so dear, and the buildup of games so out of proportion to their true importance that competitions have definitely moved away from the Coubertian ideal. This has led to a schizophrenic world where the talk is of fair play, moral values, and "what matters is to compete fairly not to win," while reality is athletes, blinded by the sight of monetary rewards and with an unbridled ego, doing whatever it takes to improve their "resume" and fans, including parent-fans, losing all manner of restraint.

Athletes need to constantly improve their resume and have no time to lose because most careers are short. They start innocuously by polishing their image. A player who scores high on name recognition is attractive for a club. Similarly, sponsors are looking as much for an image that sells as for pure performance. An attractive female Russian tennis player is worth more for them than a feisty pocket-sized Belgian one. In early 2000, Anna Kournikova's media exposure was disproportionate to her talent as a tennis player. She was receiving profitable endorsements, while Justine Henin was collecting prize money. In April 2002, Adidas admonished Anna for her poor performance on the courts; sponsors care for the right image, but this does not mean indifference to performance.

The search for an attractive resume can lead athletes to be unfaithful to a club and accept to be traded as a commodity. This can be disconcerting for spectators and fans, especially when the best players end up in a handful of rich clubs. Even the allegiance to one's country can be shed; many runners from African nations, attracted by sizeable rewards and the chance to be selected for a national team, have become citizens of Persian Gulf states.

More importantly, athletes straddle ever more the line separating fair play from outright cheating. This statement will not surprise most members of the "in-group." Fair play requires that competitors stay in full control of their emotions and win the fight against their "dark side." Most of them do not succumb to the temptation to cheat and do compete fairly. For others, pride and the prospect of large monetary gains win the battle over fairness. This leads them down various paths. They will adopt unsportsmanlike conduct. In soccer, guilty parties hardly ever acknowledge having committed a foul. Everyone claims innocence. One strategy when tackled is to fake excruciating pain, lie in agony, and miraculously heal when the referee calls a foul against the other team. In car racing, there are more elaborate techniques. The complexity of the regulations and the infinite number of small competitive advantages that can be gained by modifying the race car lead the racing teams to constantly flirt with the disallowed and, too often, to cross the line and cheat. Racecar drivers might not take drugs, but they don't mind having their cars doped.

In recent years, the most talked about attempt to distort the playing field has been the use of performance enhancing drugs. The virus spread at the end of the 20th century from cycling to track and field to soccer and more recently to baseball and even cricket. An extraordinarily telling case remains that of the East German swimmers. Their successes up to the late 80's were showcased by a harsh communist regime. After the fall of the Berlin Wall, the political will to manufacture world class athletes disappeared. No more drugs but also no more medals. When the playing field became even, the ex-East German girls were noticeably absent from the podiums by the pools.

On both sides of the Atlantic, federations, clubs, and even governments are fighting drug abuse and unsportsmanlike conduct. For the major professional sports in the U.S., it is mainly the responsibility of the commissioners of MLB, the NFL, and the NBA, and a lot rides on their success in both fights. Moral health is necessary to keep the TVs on in the family rooms on Sunday afternoons, the fathers taking their offspring to the ballpark, and the sponsors happy. Above all, the use of performance enhancing drugs can have dramatic consequences for athletes. Marco Pantani, the cyclist, had become a hero in Italy after winning the Tour of Italy and the Tour de France in 1998. A year later, he was accused of having used illegal substances and booted out of the Giro. He sank into deep depression, became addicted to cocaine, and was found dead in his room on February 14, 2004 at the age of thirty-four. He symbolizes the tragic consequences of the unbearable pressure that the media, money, fame, and fans put on athletes.

What do the fans think of these trends? On the much talked about topic of drug abuse they lament that athletes, in the world of institutionalized, entertaining, and highly competitive sport, are not virtuous and they expect unsportsmanlike behavior to pop up its ugly head now and then;

they know about drugs and cheating. In December 2004 one could read in a New York Times sport medicine page in reference to Barry Bonds and others:

"Only the naive or willfully ignorant (do) not seem to understand that drug use has been widespread for many years in elite sport."

Fans are concerned but not enough to stop attending events or watching them on television. They want the problem to be fixed and the games to go on. Their reactions after former Senator Georges J. Mitchell released his report on the use of performance-enhancing drugs in baseball on December 12, 2007 were telling. As the report presented evidence of a collective failure to acknowledge an insidious culture, the fans recognized that they were part of the "all guilty" but were quick to dedramatize the problem; they wrote curt statements such as "who cares," "let's move on," "people just want to see the game," "it's only entertainment." They don't want their dreams to be broken. How crushing when believers who have followed with enthusiasm the march of an athlete towards the breaking of a record see the results being taken off the books because the athlete cheated. But they know that cheaters need to be sanctioned. Barry Bonds beat Hank Aaron's home run record on August 7, 2007; do the fans want an "asterisk"? The answer had been given by a May 18, USA Today/Gallup Poll: only 8% of fans surveyed viewed Bonds as the greatest home run hitter ever.

The commercialization of sport and the financial transactions masterminded by the legal owners of clubs have one more impact on fans. They are concerned that it leaves them with less and less of a voice in the running of "their" club. They have a right to get upset because they do "own" the club that they support. During the course of a generation, the ownership might change several times, the players are transferred every few years and, in many cases, the club moves to a new stadium if not city. Only the community of fans remains. It is the memory, the guarantor of continuity. And the fans know that giving them their due is hardly compatible with running a club like a business.

Despite the constant patching up of its image, sport retains its popularity among the "in group" in general and hard core fans in particular. Adolescents in the U.S. consider sport participation to be the most important determinant of popularity and social status according to research reported by Dr. Christian End of the Department of Psychology at Xavier University. Adults refer to athletes as role models and cereal boxes are adorned with the faces of the most successful (Note 7). Every time the spotlight is on an athlete who has misbehaved, people will deplore the bad example that this sets for children even though social scientists say that, most presumably, parents or friends, not athletes, are the real heroes of children, the ones they are proud of and want to emulate.

Michel Caillat, a French sport psychologist, states that even though sport plays an increasingly important social role, it is not being questioned and is not the object of the extensive debates that it deserves. One of the causes is that "sport" is a generic word representing different realities. It is used to describe physical activity; jogging, biking, exercising, all qualify as doing sports and have positive connotations. Games, tennis at the local club, softball, or touch football also are being called sports; they foster competition and enthusiasm, which are positive attributes. And it is, of course, associated with institutionalized competitions. Sports as business, built on the two pillars of performance and money, benefit from the positive image of sport-physical-activity and sport-games.

Caillat has laid out the provocative argument that it is in nobody's interest to put the image of sport at risk by questioning its role in society. Who wants to debate if educational institutions are fulfilling their role in turning a blind eye to the scholastic performance of their athletes or why public funds are used to build bigger stadiums? Sport is a major economic sector; it can be part of any ideological platform; the out-group does not care and the in-group will always be protective.

Sport has more growth potential than many other economic sectors. It has room for geographical expansion. Example: Asia is a growing market for "Western" sports such as soccer and baseball; India, one day, might discover that other competitions besides cricket offer excuses for craziness (India has more than one billion inhabitants but had to wait until 2008 to collect its first Olympic gold medal; the whole country celebrated when Abhinav Bindra beat its Chinese and Finnish competitors in the final of the 10 meter air rifle). It can add "products": new sports are constantly competing for the attention of fans, to wit the "extreme" events at the Winter Olympics. Competitions are but one element of attractive entertainment packages. There are casualties now and then: the Tour de France has been seriously damaged by drug abuse and might need to be reinvented; heavyweight boxing has been lacking marquee names for too long. But the business of sport keeps renewing itself.

Where sport goes, fans follow. Growing numbers are coming from new sources, more and more women and people further away from the home town of "their" team. There will always be individuals looking for sources of identity and reasons to be enthusiastic.

✕ ✕ ✕

NOTE 5

The North American Soccer League, NASL, was started in 1967 and stopped being active in 1984.

Major League Soccer, MLS, was created around the time the U.S hosted the 1994 World Cup and became active in 1996. In 2008, fourteen teams operated in two conferences.

NOTE 6

Most of the preceding comments and specifically D. Trump's quote are taken from Brian Kilmeade's book *The Games Do Count* subtitled *America's Best and Brightest on the Power of Sports.*

NOTE 7

In 1992, the basketball player Charles Barkley caused a mini-scandal when he declared in a TV add for Nike "I am not a role model." The fact that he was not really the role model type is irrelevant. What is noteworthy is that all those with a vested interest in preserving the wholesome image of sport showed their indignation. Those in the "out group" agreed that being a famous athlete should not be confused with being the flag bearer of moral rectitude.

CHAPTER 5

"The design of a sport should allow for the decontrolling of emotions in a controlled environment."
Quest for excitement by Norbert Elias

The best chance for someone to be recognized in his community is to have a job. Society seems to have adopted the motto "tell me what you do, and I will tell you who you are." The unemployed not only lack a source of income but are isolated from the "real" world. Work can also be source of pleasure because, contrary to common belief, man is happier when he does something and work provides him with a "ready-made" environment.

Other sources of belonging and emotions are so-called leisure activities. They take place when people do not work or do not take care of their family, home or themselves. In Latin, the word for "leisure" is "otiunt," and neg-otium expresses the absence of leisure; negotiating is synonymous with working.

Leisure activities are enjoyed for their own sake and transport people into other realities (Note 8). People forget about their surroundings when they listen to a concert, watch a movie or a game. They voluntarily enter these other realms, which provide them with pleasure and excitement, opportunities to feel involved in something and to share feelings with others.

The emotions created by leisure activities can be powerful. The behavior of sport fans is well-documented but so are the idiosyncrasies of people who identify with a movie star, a rock singer, or a "diva." They too can become exuberant when luck allows them to be near the object of their passion; in the 1960's, scenes of collective madness could be observed at most of the performances of the Beatles. The joys and trials of the stars with whom they identify are also theirs; numerous magazines make sure that they do not miss any detail of the personal life of their favorite actors, actresses, and singers.

All fans are similar only up to a point. Sports fans exhibit an intensity in their behavior which is unmatched and their intransigence and inability to shed their fanhood is stunning. The reasons are found in the social role of sport and the very nature of the excitement during sports events.

SOCIAL ROLE OF SPORT

In part II of *The Civilizing Process,* written in 1939, Norbert Elias theorizes that to be civilized is to have control over one's body and emotions. Man is taught to curb his bodily expressions and the more he succeeds, the more civilized he becomes. Since the Middle Ages, how we stand in relationship to one another has changed, and these changes have had an impact on our code of conduct.

Schools of thought in Europe which can be mostly traced to the 17th century influenced how man perceives himself. The "Age of Reason" repositioned him in nature. Encouraged by Descartes's "cogito ergo sum" (Note 9) and John Locke's "we are what we become," man took center stage. To some the Enlightenment has meant primarily the emancipation from religious bigotry, to others it has been a period of broad-mindedness and sensibility; in either case, it signaled the elevation of the mind, distinct from the soul and distant from the body.

As people became more self-conscious, as they built "the invisible wall of affects which seems now to rise between one human body and another, repelling and separating" as Roy Porter writes in *Flesh In The Age Of Reason*, they developed feelings of distaste, embarrassment, or shame towards bodily functions and physical expressions of emotions. What separates acceptable manners from coarse behavior became determined externally by law and internally by reason and conscience. Roy Porter writes:

> "Vile bodies (were) consigned to their place, their subjugation reinforced through the pains and penalties of law, through training and work discipline and through stringent control of leisure and sexuality."

The changing views of the self and the refinement of manners did not affect all social classes equally. Etiquette and proper manners began at royal courts and, in a top-down process, were imitated by other social classes. This role of the courts and aristocrats would eventually be taken over by the bourgeoisie. The lower classes remained mostly on the fringe of this process. They were much less concerned with controlling flesh and didn't feel that their bodies should be considered a possible source of embarrassment. Nevertheless, by the time Queen Victoria put her imprint on England, rough and tumble cross-country games were no longer acceptable, no more free-for-alls in villages and on roads a la Ashbourne Football.

This evolution opened the door to the development of sport and its fandom. The need for exuberance and the desire to compete could not be outlawed, and the search for a conduit led to today's organized sports.

Codified games became an outlet for enthusiasm by allowing a decontrolling of emotions in a controlled environment. This theory of the social role played by sports is developed by Norbert Elias in *Quest for Excitement.* Athletes on the field are involved in battles which are allowed by the rules of the game but would not be permitted by the laws of the real world. Spectators can express their feelings in manners socially unacceptable in another space.

There was an understanding by the Greeks and the Romans that all games were war games. The history of ball games is replete with references to their use as military skill-building exercises. Today, the mimetic battle, which is at the heart of every sport, provides enjoyable excitement for the spectator. This can be achieved without negative implications for society, even though sport events can be the pretext for mob madness with dramatic consequences.

As we know, the first ones to write the rules which would allow fair competitions were college students and gentlemen in England. Schools had the fields for the required space, and at the end of the 19th century, gentlemen would consider codified games their own. The college amateur athlete was the canon; the plebeian would have to wait. His time would come, and most popular sports would eventually be associated with the lower classes. Soccer, particularly, would become the people's game and play an important role in proletarian leisure.

SPORT AND EMOTIONS
Sports competitions take place in a defined space, most of the time during a finite time period and are

conducted according to rules agreed upon by those involved. Most importantly, their object is to have a winner, and the sequence of events must remain unscripted. In a fair competition every competitor has a chance, even if small, to win; whatever the result, there are tomorrows, another opponent, and a new chance to be victorious and erase the memory of a defeat. But all the expanded energy has one overriding purpose: crowning a winner.

This represents a source of exasperating tension and therefore of intense emotions for the fans. The wait for a final result and a scenario which is fully known only at the end create a long suspense. Many games are witnessed by a large and noisy crowd which amplifies the emotions of each supporter. How fans live such an experience is best illustrated by a comparison between sports and gambling. Slot machines are programmed to deliver periodic rewards, just enough to keep the players going and the casino in the money. Those who know that they will be rewarded intermittently will pursue positive outcomes with persistence. The machine's ability to get a hold on players derives from a human feedback mechanism called "random reinforcement." Competitive sport provides the same manipulation of the human mind. The successful plays during a game, the victories throughout a season, provide the supporters with intermittent rewards.

Fans cannot escape the tension and anxiety as long as time is not up or the last batter has not struck out, but like gamblers, they are rewarded by bursts of excitement and the expectation of a positive outcome.

They remain unwilling to surrender hope when defeat looms ominously; the referee might add extra time or reset the clock and give their team a last chance. This is mere wishful thinking. Sports are not friendly tennis games where one more set to save the day cannot be refused.

LEISURE ACTIVITIES AND ENTHUSIASM

The "decontrolling" of their emotions explains the behavior of sports fans during competitions. When they identify strongly with a team/athlete, they can let their bodies and voices express their enthusiasm (Note 10).

Other leisure activities are propitious for identification and enthusiasm. They are designed around mimetism, the replication of emotions with which people are familiar. These emotions can be powerful. A movie or a concert can be filled with tension, created by scenario and acting, how the plot develops, or how electrifying the rendering of the song.

Elias Canetti, in *Crowds and Power,* Norbert Elias & Eric Dunning, in works already cited, and others have analyzed how people express their feelings during performances and why they seldom reach the intensity of emotions of sport fans during a competition. A close look at the best known of these other leisure activities reveals their predictable nature combined in most cases with restrained enthusiasm. Spectators know the broad lines of a theater show and the only surprise for the concertgoer is how the pieces will be executed; what they hear or see follows a script. These are not competitions with the nervous anticipation of a final result and most importantly, the expression of emotions must remain controlled.

Audiences at the theater, at a concert, opera, or ballet are expected to behave in a "civilized" manner. Theater shares some features with sport. Plays take place in a defined space and during a limited time period. Aristotle wrote that the proper length of a tragedy should allow the hero to pass through a series of stages from misfortune to happiness and from happiness to misfortune. Sport competitions also take place during a predetermined time period or as long as an agreed upon outcome is not reached (Note 11). A successful sport event allows competitors and spectators to pass through a series of alternating emotions, running the gamut from triumphant jubilation to misery and despair. Actors, hidden behind their disguises and only constrained by their text, can freely express their emotions and are similar to athletes who in the sanctuary of the stadium and only bound by the rules of their game, can give free rein to their exuberance. Theater spectators, though, must keep the physical expression of their enthusiasm reasonably under control. Whatever their emotions, they must observe rules of civility.

Classical music concerts create a rich palette of feelings. Leonard Bernstein taught that during the "classical" period of classical music, balance of form and shape was sought by the old stable European society, but during the Romantic Period, i.e. mostly during the 19th century, the music was meant to evoke emotions. He points to the use of sequences for excitement in symphonies and explains how the same excitement is created in sonatas by balance and contrast; the tension during the different parts is resolved at the end with a return to the tonic chord etc....This ebb and flow builds emotions, but the spectators are expected to stay even more passive than their counterparts in a theater. They must remain glued to their seats, while the conductor or soloist is highly expressive on stage. When tradition dictates that clapping is acceptable, only then can one see aficionados jumping up to shout "bravo, bravo." Few other crowds show such self-control. While a pianist or violinist is playing a piece requiring a high level of virtuosity, there is no palpable tension in the concert hall. The fallibility of an athlete is assumed. There is always nervous anticipation of the fall of ice-skaters, but few expect a musician to make mistakes. Spectators will appreciate the "sport" side of the performance but will not react as they do when watching athletes, and this does not result only from the fact that in one case mistakes are for all to see and in the other for all to hear.

The requirement for listeners to control their bodies goes back to the nineteenth century. Before the French revolution, silent listening of music or at the opera was déclassé. The change came from the rise of the bourgeoisie, applauding at specific moments signaled membership in a cultural elite.

There is more than conformity to staying put for the duration. It is also a must for the proper appreciation of classical music which requires focus during relatively long periods of time; length is a distinctive feature of the genre.

Nevertheless, every music lover knows that this self-control is a constraint which goes against nature. As the anthropologist John Blacking notes, the indivisibility of movement and sound characterizes music across cultures and times, and Daniel J.Levitin, a professor of psychology and music at McGill University, adds, music can be a more satisfying experience if we let it move us physically.

Opera is music and theater. Its fans share behavioral and character traits with sport fans. They are aware of the presence of the tenor or soprano on stage, of their physical performance; they know if a voice has been successful in testing its limits. Sopranos expect to be elevated to the rank of divas; tenors are not far behind the top of the ego scale. Opera fans root for their favorites, are very knowledgeable about the arias, how they have been performed and have their memories. Aficionados are known to express their disappointment by booing marquee names. When this happens, it makes the news as it did when Roberto Alagna left the stage at the Scala in Milan in December 2006 after being booed for his performance of the first aria of *Aida*. But such behavior is frowned upon. The line in the sand drawn by society beyond which fans at sport competitions enter a "controlled environment for decontrolled feelings" is not to be crossed lightly in other leisure activities.

There are well recorded exceptions to this rule as even the most "controlled" crowds indulge from time to time in uncivilized behavior. The histories of theater, dance, and music feature celebrated cases of rowdy partisanship. Victor Hugo wrote a play entitled *Hernani,* which was meant to extol Romantic ideals as opposed to the Classical, which dominated the stage at the time. The premiere, on February 25, 1830, ended up being a tumultuous affair, which pitted the partisans of both styles against each other. For the two months thereafter, the play was interrupted night after night by the audience. It is remembered as the "Battle of Hernani." A similar demonstration of partisanship took place on May 29, 1913 when *The Rite of Spring* composed by Igor Stravinsky was performed by Les Ballets Russes in Paris. The rhythmic score and the depiction of pagan scenes unsettled the spectators accustomed to the conventions of classical ballet. The unrest degenerated to fights and the police had to reestablish order at intermission. Such outbreaks can be expected when the canons of an art form are being challenged and are colorful and infrequent exceptions to civilized behavior.

Physical restraint is not expected at rock or pop concerts. Dense masses, mostly in large open spaces, are there to give free rein to their emotions. Their exuberance is amplified by the sight and noise of others in the crowd. They have a liberating experience. When Madonna is performing, she fills the space with energy, and all her fans are in ecstasy.

My daughter, France, a former fan of jam bands, makes the point that their concerts have some of the ingredients that make a sport competition exciting. Young people come for the togetherness and the remembering. They identify with the stars. Tension builds up as a "jam" progresses towards a climactic point and then is released. Musicians and athletes, aware of the crowd's emotions, know how to build excitement. The soloist improvising and adding another meaning to the piece creates the same surprising joy as an athlete making a brilliant move that is not in the playbook. There is anticipation and recollection of tunes and plays, sometimes disappointment when the performers are not at the top of their game, and of course, sound, by waves, acts as the connective tissue, bringing everybody together at the concert or in the stadium. In both places, the display of enthusiasm is permitted, but rock concerts are not competitions with winners and losers. And neither are pop concerts. There is no dreaded or willed result that keeps spectators on edge. There is, to be sure, disappointment and pleasure during the performances, but even if the crowd can reach high levels of jubilation, it never falls into despair (Note 12).

Movies can match the emotions experienced at sport events. Spectators in a cinema are hypnotized by the images on the screen. Many scenarios take the spectators through a gamut of emotions and some have unexpected twists. *The Crying Game* or *Million Dollar Baby* had elements of surprise of such magnitude that the critics were shackled in writing their reviews since they could not disclose the ending of the films. Movies can also leave psychological scars. I am but one of many who recall being anxious outdoors after having seen Alfred Hitchcock's *The Birds* and to whom the backcountry of Georgia evokes frightening scenes from *Deliverance*. Movie fans do carry memories of a show and refer to it for years, but in the movie house, they are part of a fairly passive crowd. They do not have the liberating experience of the sport fan in a stadium.

Despite having different experiences during performances, fans of movies and of sports have numerous similarities. Actors and actresses offer a rich and broad terrain for fandom. Their fans identify with them as sport fans do with athletes, and both groups try to have an intimate knowledge of the lives of their idols. They remember all the facts and figures. Movie fans can recite who played in what and with whom in the same way that sport fans show off their grasp of who scored, when, and where. Each activity offers escape and hope to its followers. Adolescents will try to walk in the footsteps of their heroes, dreaming of a successful career in the majors or in Hollywood. Most of them have to fall back on copying the look of an actress or wearing the name of an athlete on their tee-shirt. Sports and movie fans sometimes lose track of the line dividing fantasy and reality and can no longer move freely between the two domains. Those searching for an identity always run the risk of becoming alienated, and this is particularly true for highly identified cinema and sport fans.

Sound adds depth to emotions. The newest slot machines use sight and sound—bursts of music that get louder the deeper a player gets into a game—all designed to amplify excitement. The action on a movie screen is announced and enhanced by the music, to the greatest satisfaction of the spectators. No Alfred Hitchcock movie would convey the same restlessness and anticipation without the music composed by Bernard Herrmann, one of the first musicians to create orchestral color appropriate to the particular narrative of a movie. It is his use of volume and rhythm which adds relief to Orson Welles's *Citizen Kane*. One of the most well known marriages of music and film is *The Pink Panther*. Henry Mancini's theme always brings forth images of the big cat.

Spectators at sport competitions are free to be noisy, to cheer, and to sing. Elias Canetti theorized that noise transforms a mass of spectators into a crowd. Sound is an essential element of the excitement generated by competitions and adds to the drama on the field. Sport spectators know about the indivisibility of movement and sound noted by John Blacking in relation to music. Cheering makes them experience physically the rhythm of the action; they enter the game and become active participants. They also know that their chants provide fuel to the players and that noise can become a real handicap for the visiting team. Fans are part of the "home field advantage." During American football games, commentators are quick to acknowledge that the noise level has interfered with the call of the play on a critical down for the visitors. When the defense of the home team prevails, they can be heard to say, "They owe this one to the crowd." This active role played by the home crowd can even have a perverse effect. Researchers from Harvard University analyzed statistical data, mainly goals scored, from a long series of games played in the English Premier Soccer league and claim to have demonstrated scientifically that home fans induce a subconscious bias in referees. There is no doubt that the psychological pressure by an omnipresent, noisy, and hostile crowd can have an influence on a referee's decisions and that a bias can also result from his fear of bodily harm, during and mostly after the game.

Long before these scientific data were published, academics suggested that the presence of spectators in a stadium renders the playing field uneven and therefore makes true fair play impossible. They imagined games played without the presence of spectators with a crowd watching the action on giant screens elsewhere. Similarly, aficionados of old time movies considered that real cinema is without music. More recently, some film directors have felt that the sound was giving too much away of the upcoming action on the screen;

spectators are being guided by the score because the music is flagging what is going to happen. These views are intellectually stimulating and useful in reflecting on what movies and sports events are all about, but reality is that even if sound distracts from the image and the narrative flow or handicaps fair play, spectators want to be in a total "happening": the drama on the field amplified by the noise of the crowd, the power of the image reinforced by the music of the film.

The enjoyment of competitions is enhanced by surprises. There is little pleasure in a one-sided game when skill and chance favor only one of the competitors. After the 2000 season, Ferrari and Michael Schumacher became an unbeatable team and seemed to be putting Formula 1 racing on its death-bed. Too much perfection, too much predictability, took the tension out of the races. Fortunately, thanks partly to new rules, a different team became "the unbeatable one" in 2005, and Formula 1 racing goes on. Does this mean that frequently recurring victories by a competitor are detrimental to the dynamics of a sport? In the literature on sports fandom, one finds repeatedly statements such as: "although team performance is clearly important for highly identified persons, the main reason for being a fan is based on the activity itself." In other words, the casual fan doesn't mind "intermittent rewards," but the partisan spectator wants success and has no use for defeat. Just like athletes who have kept the agonostic spirit of the Greeks, the love to compete but also to win, true fans share philonikia, the love of victory.

Committed fans of winning teams want nothing else than the comfort of success. They leave the excitement of intermittent rewards to sport commentators and fans of other teams. New York Yankees fans, up to a few years ago, did not look for intermittent rewards. Their baseball team had ended the 2004 regular season by winning their 7th consecutive division title. To every fan's surprise their record in early May 2005 stood at a dismal 11 wins-19 losses. It improved to 39-39 by July 1st, but on September 10, they still trailed the division-leading Red Sox by four games. In full disregard of a tradition of regular season successes, they were in danger of missing the playoffs. This was a season filled with tension for true fans of the New York Yankees. How did they react? They did not enjoy this departure from the routine of previous seasons meant only to prepare their team for the championship games. They did not care for the tension during each game, the reversal of fortunes, the successions of exaltation and despair. They were the fans of a dominant team and didn't want it any other way. The Yankees did win their division but lost in the first round of the playoffs.

The fans must have known that they had good reasons to be on edge. In 2006 and 2007, the Yankees did not make it past the first round of their division series, and they did not even make the playoffs in 2008. Maybe their fans will have to rethink their sense of entitlement and learn to enjoy intermittent rewards.

Fans of less successful teams have to play with the hand that fate has dealt them. When they identify with a recurring contender, they have learned to cope with the disappointments of seasons that could have been, like Red Sox fans whose team won the World Series Championship in 2004 after a wait of eighty-six years. They convinced themselves that victory is so much sweeter if it is long in coming. But they did win again in 2007, so do young Red Sox fans now have a sense of entitlement?

There are also die-hard fans of endemically losing teams who continue to watch their team run long strings of defeats; they don't expect victories, so they seek rewards elsewhere, in reinforced faithfulness for some, in derogatory language for others.

It is well-established that numerous leisure activities are a fertile ground for spectator excitement, that they allow identification with heroes, create tension and tease with random reinforcement of hope; the presence of crowds and sound can intensify emotions, and the experience of some fans is heightened by their memories. It can be convincingly argued that, among all these activities, sports events are the most powerful source of enthusiasm. The features that tip the scale in their favor are the socially acceptable "decontrolling" of emotions during competitions combined with the unscripted nature of events and the anxious anticipation of the outcome.

The sport fan is kept on the edge of his seat by the knowledge that the greatest athlete can always be beaten by someone more driven. Experience has also taught him that the final outcome can be dictated by chance even in the face of superior merit. He can never rely on the conviction that his team is intrinsically the best. This as much as any other feature makes sports a source of drama and excitement. It might also explain why Americans respond particularly well to the stimulation of sports. The cultural historian Jackson Lears wrote that America's sense of destiny is defined by two archetypes: the self-made man, who believes in the power of his own work, and the gambler, who believes in providence. Sport competitions remind the U.S. fans of the tension in their real lives between hard work and good fortune.

MEMORIES OF THE TOUR.

When I was a teenager, neither my family nor any of my friends had a television set in their house. Radio and the local newspaper were our sources of information on what was going on in the world of sport. I was interested in soccer but also, every summer, fascinated by the Tour de France.

The first American to win a stage was Greg Lemond in 1985 and the average American discovered the Tour in the 90's, but it was present in my life forty years earlier. Besancon, my home town, was sometimes a stop-over town. I was familiar with the feel of the "caravan" and still recall the sight of the competitors at the end of the stage, their faces and limbs deeply tanned but revealing pale torsos when they changed their jerseys. The equipment was primitive; riders carried a spare inner tube like a backpack and used pedal clips. The purses were modest. The physical performance, though, was exciting. On most July afternoons, I would expectantly listen to the reporting on the day's stage. There was nervous anticipation as I waited to hear the name of the first one to reach the summits in the Alps or the Pyrenees. Riders were defending the colors of their country, and there were epic battles between the heroes of Italy, France, and a handful of other European nations. There was no need for TV "hype" to generate enthusiasm and to leave me with lasting memories.

While discussing this book with an old friend of mine, I was surprised to learn that the yearly bike race had been his introduction to the world of sport. After a friendship of close to forty years, Eric told me how as a teenager he would avoid the boredom of summer Sunday lunches by sneaking out of the family room and listening to the Tour on the radio.

In recent years, the Tour has been devastated by drug abuse. It was made into a farce in 2007; while it was supposed to be on the mend, it seemed to collapse under the weight of the daily expulsion of top names. Why should one continue to show interest in it?

The Tour belongs in a book where sport is presented as a source of enthusiasm. Since its beginnings, it has been a media event and has entertained millions along the roads of France. At the turn of the 20ᵗʰ century, a man called Henri Desgrange, a contemporary of Pierre de Coubertin, launched a newspaper, "L'Auto-Velo," and shared the cycling readership with another paper, "Le Velo." In search of a competitive advantage, he endorsed the suggestion of a journal reporter to sponsor a bicycle race around France. The first Tour started on July 1ˢᵗ 1903, financed by the media and companies with interest in tires and bikes; ever since, the Tour de France has been operated by private companies.

A friend of mine from business school, Jean Francois Naquet-Radiguet, was, nearly twenty years ago, the general manager of the Tour in charge of business and communication. He very graciously gave me the opportunity to get an inside view.

I learned about that side of the Tour that the public knows the least, the well-oiled machine that has operated successfully over the years. In many respects, it lacked professionalism before Jean Francois's days but since then has become more efficient, particularly in its relationship with sponsors, television, and other media.

Now and then during our meeting, Jean Francois did refer to the drug scandal. It is well known that the Tour and performance enhancers have been together for a long time. A rider from decades ago, presumably Jacques Anquetil, the winner of five Tours in 1957 and 1961 to 64, has said something like, "Did you expect us to make it to the top of the mountains on Perrier alone?" In the last ten years, though, the connection has become embarrassingly close. The progress made by science has presented temptations that too many have not resisted. So-called doctors and advisers have come up with more and more magic tricks, and riders don't seem to be able to avoid sliding down the slope leading to doping. The same can be said about many other institutionalized sports, but the problem is painfully endemic and visible in cycling.

The old ways of tracking cheaters, say analyzing urine and blood samples at the end of a stage, are not keeping pace with the sophistication of cheaters and their teams of scientists. But there is hope. Thanks to new technologies riders who used drugs have been caught several months after the end of the 2008 Tour. On and off controls may have to be replaced by a monitoring of biological data over a long period. The International Cycling Federation, ICF, took an encouraging step when it required riders to have such a "biological passport" since the beginning of 2008. The cooperation between the ICF and the Tour organizer, Amaury Sport Organisation, will have to be redefined. In any case, to paraphrase Jean Francois, the Tour will have to be reinvented.

Much will need to be done to reestablish a sense of fair play and credibility in the achievements of the riders and to protect their health. This is critical because spectators and fans are seeking not only the carnival atmosphere but the extremes of the physical performance. The men climbing steep mountains and reaching stunning speeds during time trials are admired for sweat, tears, and suffering. A study done in the spring of 2002 indicated that spectators did not care for "robocops" and were enthusiastic about riders who knew how to suffer on the roads of the Tour. Fans seek unscripted stages run by athletes who test their limits.

Some people doubt that the Tour can survive, but I side with the optimists. It is so much more than a bike race. It is a yearly event, and as Nicolas Sarkozy, the French President, said, "A month of July without the Tour de France would not be a month of July." It is to France what baseball is to the U.S. Any American president could paraphrase Sarkozy: "A summer without baseball would not be a summer." Both activities are steeped in memories. Fans recall highly emotional moments, clutch hits, and costly errors for some, fascinating chases up winding mountain roads for others.

I am sure Jean Francois Naquet-Radiguet could have talked for hours about the next steps for the Tour. But this was not why I had asked to meet with him. Half way through our conversation, I had heard the words that I was hoping he would say: nostalgia, celebration, and beauty. The recollection of exploits of riders, the carnival atmosphere of the so-called caravan, and the majesty of the French countryside, all defining features of the Tour.

An article in the June 7, 2007 edition of the New York Times Sports Magazine said, referring to the theatrical series of drug scandals, "All of which leaves us in a dilemma, do we pass grim judgment or sit back on July 07 with a cold sauvignon blanc and toast the world's most grueling, beautiful, unbelievable race? We have made our choice. "A votre sante!"

Despite more scandals during the race, I did join the toasters in 2007 and 2008 and hope to do this for years to come.

ЖЖЖ

NOTE 8

The English word "school" is derived from the Greek *schole,* which was used to designate leisure, and not surprisingly, *askolia* was used for work. During the Classical period in Greece, around the 4th century BC, the same free men who went to the gymnasium to exercise their body also had time to study, perhaps to listen to Aristotle on the grounds of the Lyceum in Athens. For them studying was a pleasure. Leisure gave them time to learn things that are for their own sake, to contemplate. And Aristotle would relate sport to contemplation as each is "for its own sake."

NOTE 9

From the writings of Pope Jean Paul II:

"For Descartes, ESSE (to be) was of secondary importance, while he considered COGNOSCO (I know) to be primordial. Man is left alone to decide what is good and what is bad. God only belonged in human conscience; he could no longer be considered the One who explains the depth of human's SUM (I am)."

NOTE 10

It must be remembered that "to identify with" means becoming the same as, adopting the identity of, someone else and that things having to do with identity matter to fans.

NOTE 11

Soccer is played during ninety minutes plus stoppage time and eventually overtime. A winner in tennis is declared after a certain number of sets, and the match has no time limit. In some competitions, "time" is a critical element of the game being played. Intelligent use of the clock towards the end of an American football game can mean the difference between victory and defeat. In 2005, at the end of a long summer of cricket, rain delays played a decisive role in Australia, handing over to England the Ashes, the trophy so passionately fought for by these two countries every two years.

NOTE 12

This is mostly true. Some genres of music can create moods in the audience that are more extreme than others. For instance, cognoscenti will say that "Heavy Metal" music infuses anger and aggression in a crowd.

CHAPTER 6

"Because of the increased importance highly identified fans place on their team's performance, their affective, cognitive and behavioral reaction tends to be quite extreme."

Sport Fans by Daniel L. Wann.

September 2, 1972 saw a full day of track and field at the Olympia stadium in Munich. The mood was festive. The Olympic Games had not yet been marred by the massacres that would send the world into mourning a few days later. The 400 meter hurdles was one of the afternoon events, not highly anticipated even though it is always a show of speed, endurance, and skill. Shortly after the race had reached its mid-point, one athlete took the lead and stride by stride extended it. He was not the favorite, but the crowd started chanting his name "Akii-Bua, Akii-Bua…" The sight of this superb athlete gliding above the hurdles and exhibiting such mastery exalted the crowd. Everybody was on their feet, and the rhythmic chant of the four syllables continued as he victoriously crossed the finish line. He would take a victory lap, draped in the flag of his country, Uganda. The crowd knew that it had witnessed a memorable event. He was the gold medalist and had broken the world record.

Thirty-six years later, I still hear the chant of "Akii-Bua" and feel the excitement that I shared with those around me in the stadium. We experienced such enthusiasm and built lasting memories even though I doubt that many of us had a particular connection to the athlete who captivated us that day.

Sport inspires emotions even to the occasional spectator, and to the people attached to a team or an athlete it brings excitement, joy, and despair.

Fans come from all walks of life without distinction of race, gender, or social class and can be found in a variety of places. At the end of the 90's, when French soccer was at a pinnacle, many members of the national team were playing in the English "Premiership," the major league. The French ambassador to England, Daniel Bernard, was well aware of this and knew that a reception at his residence would be even more successful if he invited French players from Chelsea or Arsenal. Some members of the House of Lords would not miss a chance to commingle with the soccer stars du jour while sipping champagne and eating canapés.

In another part of the world, fans of the University of Alabama football team, the Crimson Tide, can be observed in their motor homes in the parking lots surrounding the stadiums of the Southeastern Conference teams. The lively book written by Warren St John, *Rammer, Jammer, Yellow Hammer*, tells stories about fans driving from game to game in their RVs, congregating around the stadium several days before kickoff and indulging in comfortable four star tailgating.

Other tailgaters can be seen in parking lots of professional football stadiums all over the U.S. on game day. They come early, unfold a few chairs and a table, and fire up the grill. A la carte will be hot dogs and hamburgers served with beer. They toss a football around and have a pleasurable experience equal in importance to the upcoming game.

True fans form a community. People who otherwise have little in common share a passion. Whatever their resume, they can be observed becoming excessively excited at the sight of performing athletes, being boisterous and noisy, talking a lot, and bragging if possible. They sometimes rub elbows in a stadium but most of the time are physically dispersed and connected only by the memories, hopes, and addictions that they share.

The reputation of a sports fan has a lot to do with how much he knows and more precisely, how authoritative he appears. The National Football League draft is a good illustration of the importance of being in the know. It is an annual televised event, and its audience keeps growing. The drama on the screen unfolds as the representatives of each NFL team pick from the eligible crop of collegiate talent. The process, which involves several rounds, lasts from Saturday noon to Sunday afternoon usually during the last week end in April. Endless streams of information on potential future star players are distilled. For those involved in gambling and fantasy teams it is nothing more than doing their homework, but countless other fans are obsessive about the draft because it satisfies their need for data and role playing. The emotional energy invested during that one weekend allows them to display their knowledge in front of other fans during the football season (Note 13).

People who don their fan mantles withdraw from their ordinary world and become captivated, some would say mesmerized, by the sport events that they witness. They feel comfortable in this other world, and it brings them pleasure. There, they think of nothing but the competition taking place. Almost any discipline will give them access to this other reality. This is why they are easy prey for the sports media as can be observed during Olympic Games, better even Winter Olympic Games. Every four years, for a few days, sports fans will develop a genuine appreciation for little-known disciplines, like luge or curling. They will enjoy the competitions, share the excitement of the television commentators, and even claim to understand the fine points of these sports. At the end of the Games, they will redirect their passion to college basketball or hockey unless while zapping they decide to stop on a channel showing Australian rule football. Fans enjoy this world that most of them enter and withdraw from at will. They find comfort in this other universe because of its non-compulsory, it's "for its own sake" nature.

The involvement of fans can be more or less intense. Most of them will be satisfied to watch games on television or treat themselves to an occasional outing at the stadium. There, they will cheer for "their" team and join the roar of the crowd during the ebb and flow of the contest. When the game is over, they will talk about it, showing off knowledge, and then they will look forward to the next competition. They are the largest group, serious but not excessive.

Some of the more committed ones belong to fan communities, "clubs" for instance. With the ease of communication offered by the Internet, staying attuned to the activities of an organization has become ever easier. Team fan clubs take different forms and serve various functions: information on the team and upcoming events, focal points for geographically dispersed supporters, discussion forums or Internet chatting. They might provide social activities, organize games for young players, and fund raising. In the U.S., few make serious attempts to have a say in the management of the team. In England and on the Continent, some have strong leadership and represent the fans in discussions with the club owners and management. Such fan clubs are often the emanation of a local community or represent a section of a town and have features that reflect the local history and geography.

The most intense fans are the "highly identified fans," the HIF, a term commonly used in academic literature. Their life experiences have led to strong bonds with athletes or teams, and they are the most profoundly alienated. They struggle to keep a dividing line between their real world and this other reality, the world of sport from which they do not withdraw at will.

In May 2007, *The Arizona Republic* reported that the last words of a man put to death by lethal injection had been "Go Raiders," the war cry of the fans of the Oakland football team. What is one to make of such stunning behavior? Was it defiance towards the witnesses of his execution? A sign that fans live in another world which, when called for, overpowers their real world? Is this story macabre or sad, sad that a man cannot find anything better to say when his life is coming to an end?

The HIF exhibit the character traits of all sport fans, the excessiveness and the passion. Their behavior is influenced by what happens to "their" team, their mood colored by the result of each competition. They do have a distinctive feature: they need to protect their self-image and image in their community because their identification is a building block of their identity, hence their intensity.

Each competition is a renewed challenge. The preparation for a game is an attempt to exorcise the demons of defeat. The HIF have a list of incantations which will help carry their team to victory. They will wear good luck outfits and become the true soul mates of the athletes who have good luck socks, gloves, and caps or look for heavenly protection by wearing religious medals. Some HIF, in an even more powerful gesture, will not watch some games because they believe that their team seldom loses when they learn the score only long after the game is over. Others simply cannot take the pressure and never watch their favorite teams play, savoring the replays when the result is in their favor.

When victory is on their side, they proudly claim it as their own. Their mood receives a jolt, energy flows, and they face the real world with a smile on their faces. The academics call this mental state basking in reflected glory. It is in defeat that they are the most fragile because they are powerless. They feel sorry for themselves, but there is no escape. When their hopes are about to be crushed, they can only take the pain. Their body language, hands behind the neck like prisoners of fate, says it all.

After a loss, the HIF will fantasize about what could and should have happened, recall more glorious days, and manipulate facts and figures to help cope with their threatened identity. They try to reduce what the social psychologist Leon Festinger in his 1957 book on this subject called their "cognitive dissonance." When facts do not fit with feelings, people try to find a way to reconcile them. Anyone can be led to do this, drinkers who pretend that alcohol is good for their health, smokers who do not believe in the risk of secondhand smoke, parents at sports events who are convinced that the referee is biased against their children and of course, the HIFs (Note 14).

On Monday morning, they will call their local sports radio station, speak like the coach, the owner, or the athlete with whom they identify and prepare themselves mentally for the next game. Victory and exaltation are only a few strokes of luck away. Their lives as fans goes on, each game creating more memories and adding to the thread that binds them to their pasts. There is always another game, always possible redemption, always hope. They know that they must bear defeats in the hope of being ultimately rewarded by victories.

A few, now and then, try to give up. In an article in the *New York Times* in January 2004, titled "A Fan Throws in The Towel and Hangs up His Spikes," a journalist relates how he couldn't do it anymore; it was becoming too taxing. It was good fun journalism but in the end just an empty threat. Real fans can't break the bonds and erase the memories.

Alain Cayzac and I knew each other when we studied at HEC, a business school in Paris, in the early sixties. He played on the college soccer team and while still a young man became one of the founding fathers of Paris-Saint-Germain, PSG, the first division Paris soccer team. He has been involved with this club throughout most of his life in various capacities. For many years, he was one of the top executives at Havas, a worldwide advertising firm, conducting his business affairs with the poise and savvy that one acquires after years in communication. He has a firm handle on his children, proud to see his sons also committed fans of PSG. In April 2006, after the club was bought out by a trio of investors, some of whom associated with American investment firms, he was asked to become the president of the club. Two years later, he resigned, unable to carry any longer the weight of PSG's dramatically poor performances. A sad episode in the life of someone who so loves his club.

I had met with Alain in September 2005 to tell him about my project. As he remarked, he should be the one writing his memoirs instead of me trying to conduct an interview. His first comments were on the topic of hooliganism, as if this was an obvious start. He has had to acquire over the years an understanding of this dreaded type of fan behavior and how clubs, particularly the PSG, must develop strategies to deal with them. What I learned that day is referenced in the next chapter.

His other relevant remarks were about his life as an HIF. He rarely misses a game and was candid in admitting that when he enters that part of his world he loses all control over his emotions. He becomes excessive in his physical behavior and verbally abusive towards whomever he thinks stands in the way of his team's victory. After certain games, when victory had been within reach only to be denied by cruel reversals of fortunes, he needs the help of friends or family to release the tension that built in him during the ninety or more minutes of the competition.

Cayzac's case is one of many to be found in the world of sport where leaders in the fields of business, academics or politics become irrational, biased, and blinded by their fanhood. How can they lose control over their passions so easily and abruptly when sport is concerned? How can men harbor such extreme personae? How can they switch from one behavior mode to another without apparent continuity?

People in today's society face a large diversity of social situations. Family man, consumer, employee or employer, registered voter, sports fan, etc... man must be multifaceted. He lives in a plurality of worlds which have different cognition rules. His cultural background and the groups to which he belongs will determine how he reacts and his modes of action in each of these worlds. He appears to have discontinuous behavior patterns when he is in alternating realities, but most psychologists and sociologists will say that despite apparent mutations of identity, a fundamental coherence remains.

The world of sport fandom is filled with intense emotions, and in the intimacy of his home or in a public place surrounded by other spectators, the fan is free to express boundless enthusiasm. This explains why a man of reason, Alain the businessman, can become abruptly a man of uncontrolled passion, Alain the PSG fan.

NOTE 13

"Fantasy teams" involve real athletes in a virtual environment, a symbiosis of sport and gambling. Most committed fans are gamblers; it goes with the turf. Selecting a fantasy team is a way of exhibiting one's knowledge of the game, of getting involved. It is a small compensation for dedicated fans who otherwise are passive, albeit noisy, actors. The competition is not for real, but the results are because the winners acquire real bragging rights on top of monetary gains. Fantasy leagues also build traditions. Some of them were created when the participants were young adolescents, and have allowed them to stay connected as adults.

NOTE 14

The concept of "cognitive dissonance" is now an analytical tool used by many disciplines. Finance is one.

Economic agents do not always behave rationally when they are given new information. This leads to inefficiencies in asset pricing. Behavioral finance analyzes the psychological phenomena which can lead to mispricing. It is in this context that cognitive dissonance can provide a framework in which biased reactions to news can be explained.

CHAPTER 7

"Carnival supporters display sociable, gregarious and boisterous behavior, Hooligan ones engage in competitive violence with other fan groups."
Behavior types of sport crowds presented in <u>Fanatics</u>, a collection of essays edited by Adam Brown.

The behavior of a fan takes on higher levels of intensity when he is in a crowd. A sport crowd can have different morphologies. It can be small when supporters gather in a bar, dispersed over long distances, thousands of spectators lining roads to watch the Tour de France or a "psychological crowd," fans connected by the flow of information that they are eager to capture on specialized radio, television stations, in the press, and on the internet. The typical sport crowd, though, the one most people from the in-group as well as the out-group think of, is a very large group of people rubbing elbows in a stadium. Americans will recall an aerial view of The Rose Bowl Stadium in Pasadena, California, and Europeans, the tightly packed "Camp Nou" soccer stadium in Barcelona. A closer observation reveals a high level of collective excitement, spontaneous releases of energy, a mass united by chants which express great joy but can quickly turn into threatening roars. The mood is that of a carnival but can become that of a riot.

THE SPORT FAN IN A CROWD.

The behavior of crowds and what happens to people in a crowd is the subject of crowd psychology. The scholarship goes back to the very end of the 19ᵗʰ century when the name most commonly associated with this field was Gustave Le Bon who wrote *Crowd Psychology* in 1895, a book still used as a reference on the topic. (Appendix 2 gives a short synopsis of the history of crowd psychology and a summary of Le Bon's theories). One of his fundamental assumptions was that when a gathering becomes a crowd, people lose their individuality and form a collective spirit. It is reflected in the adjectives used to describe man in a crowd: anonymous, lost, primitive, etc…

Le Bon's views are still relied upon to explain and to a certain point absolve the behavior of rowdy fans. Writings on sports spectators do make regular reference to his theories either implicitly or explicitly (Note 15).

There are many reasons for the longevity and popularity of Le Bon's theories, not the least of which their attractiveness to right wing politicians and fascist dictators; a theory that crowds are irrational is helpful to propagate that strong leadership is necessary.

Nevertheless, the study of crowds has moved on during the 20ᵗʰ century. Historians have looked at what George Rude called "faces in the crowd" and at the motivations of individuals, and sociologists have developed new concepts. One of these, the "social identity theory" is particularly applicable to the understanding of large gatherings at sport events. It stresses the interaction that takes place between groups that form a crowd instead of focusing on the crowd as a whole or on individuals in particular and suggests that a spectator in a stadium does not become anonymous but instead a member of a subgroup. People surrender their personal identity to the social identity of that group and their behavior is intensified.

This post-Le Bon theory also posits that a crowd does not have a "soul"; its behavior is only the sum of the behavior of each individual (Note 16).

In a stadium, fans sit among the members of their tribe. There are no good reasons to be elsewhere if they want to enjoy the experience. Surrounded by their peers they find pleasure in freely expressing their emotions and are stimulated by the sight of others sharing their passions. They feel less inhibited and become the actors in a show being watched by other spectators who in turn become actors.

People who attend football or soccer games are familiar with the notion of subgroups inside of a crowd. Spectators wearing the colors of their team help map the space. It is easy to spot the tight-knit groups of supporters of the visitors and the boisterous ones of the local team, very vocal and often led in songs by well-known fans. These subgroups are circumstantial and only cemented by the expression of the emotions shared by their members. When they come together, they form a crowd.

Elias Canetti in *Crowds and Power*, written in 1960, describes how masses of people become a crowd and the importance of sound in the process. He calls the spectators at a sport event a stagnant mass, i.e. a compact and expectant crowd. In a stadium, they have little freedom of movement and are together up to the end of the event, hence the reference to "stagnant." They are not passive, though, as they are free to let their voices and bodies express emotions (Note 17). NFL teams often have unofficial mascots, mostly in outrageous costumes, whose role is to excite the crowd. The roar, songs, chants, and vocal rituals in a stadium are the voice of the crowd and unite all the spectators.

When they are not in the same physical space, fans still belong to a type of crowd, sharing a psychological space. Wherever they are, at home in front of their TV set or listening to a game on their car radio, they form a crowd. They are united by their hopes, memories, and the knowledge that other fans are simultaneously experiencing similar emotions.

"CARNIVAL" CROWDS

Physical crowds of sport fans have behavioral styles. The most common one is referred to as "Carnival," an appropriate qualifier as it expresses both the festive and fantasy nature of such masses of spectators. "Carnivals" are the festivals that take place before the beginning of Lent (from the Latin carne and levare, the time when one does not eat meat). They are explosions of license and call for disguises, a necessary condition to feel free to commit excesses. The wearing of a mask during Carnival liberates one from the prudence and reserve that must be observed the rest of the year. In a crowd of sport spectators, the mask of the fans is the group to which they belong. A Carnival atmosphere is the product of all the psychological features and behavioral idiosyncrasies described throughout this book. The passions of people who identify with a sport/team /athlete, the tension created by the ebb and flow of the action, the low level of self-control which amplifies the expression of emotions, the deafening sound, the exaltation of victory and the despair of defeat, all come together and find their ultimate expression in this carnival atmosphere.

A good place to experience it is at a college football game on an early winter Saturday afternoon. Fans with painted faces, headgear, naked torsos, particularly a propos in sub-zero weather, waving signs, sometimes humorous, and banners, are scattered in a sea of other fans bearing the colors of their school. They join in songs and noises, emoting as loudly as they can. At the end of the game, they might invade the playing field, succumb to collective madness, and tear down goal posts. Later, in the streets around the stadium, too many cans of beer will lower their level of self-control to unsafe levels, free their tongues to denigrate the rival of the day, but the door is rarely open to excessive destructiveness. Incidentally, a recent Harvard School of Public Health College Alcohol Study shows that more sports fans students binge drink and have alcohol-related problems than non-fan students.

"Carnival" behavior is mostly non-violent, even when associated with heavy consumption of alcohol. It can be boisterous but is mostly sociable and characterizes the atmosphere not only at college and high school games but also during team sports events in general.

"HOOLIGAN" CROWDS

Even though the typical sports fan manages his or her emotions admirably, as Allen Guttman writes in *Sports Spectators,* there is unfortunately a "hooligan" style of behavior. A lot of attention is paid, mostly by members of the out-group, to the spectacular exactions of this minority of destructive and violent fans.

The term "hooligan" is said to have its origin in the asocial behavior of a family, the Hooligans, during a rebellion in Ireland at the end of the 19th century and qualifies behavior which is threatening, violent, and demonizing of "the other."

Most violent incidents occurring during sport events are tied to groups, and cases of individuals acting on their own such as the attacker of Monica Seles or the killer of a Columbian soccer player who had scored a goal against his own team during the 1994 Soccer World cup are rare.

The term hooliganism can be used to qualify violent crowd behavior at any type of sport event, but it is mostly associated with soccer. Scenes of violence involving fan groups with a fearful reputation were recurring in England in the 1980's; "firms" of Chelsea and Leeds were notorious. The most dramatic incident took place in May 1985 when Liverpool fans caused the death of thirty-nine people, mostly supporters of the Italian club Juventus, at the Heysel Stadium in Brussels during the European Cup Final. A year earlier, Liverpool had won the Cup by beating AS Roma, in Rome, and after the game, Italian fans had attacked the celebrating Liverpool fans. Before the start of the 1985 final, supporters of the English club charged; Juventus fans, lacking an escape route, were crushed against the rear of a terrace, a wall of the stadium gave way and people could not avoid the ensuing stampede. In reaction to the Heysel tragedy, the UEFA, the European Soccer Union, banned English clubs for a short time from European competitions.

The commercialization of soccer, the changes in the configuration of stadiums and increased security have resulted in a reduction of violence in England in recent years. The problem, though, remains critical for soccer federations elsewhere in Europe, Italy being the current bad boy. Actions, there, are planned by "brigades." During the 2002–2003 season, the security measures taken each day when games of the Italian soccer league, the Calcio, were played, cost the state thirty-two million euros. During the same year twenty-eight policemen on average were injured on each of those days.

Hooligans polluting soccer games are bound to each other by strong ties, have a common history, and are sensitive to the reputation of their tribe. They fight for the colors of their club and sometimes control one of its Fan Clubs. They express their partisanship by theatricalizing violence. Hooligans are fans, but violence gives them social visibility and sets them apart from other supporters. The games played by their team provide the opportunity for scripted actions, which follow known rules and codes. The goal is to defend the reputation of their "firm," intimidate the other tribe and win the battle of the day.

They will play "games," inside as well as outside of the stadium. The threat of violence will always be present and, in most cases, the hooligan tribe will not resist the appeal of the highs of actual violence and destructiveness. Its reputation as an alpha group is being tested during away games and even more so when there is a longstanding war with the rival of the day. The collective ego dictates that they show no fear and leave the battle field with honor.

Members of the home team "firm" will gather before the game, mostly at pubs and march to the stadium in formations reminiscent of a Greek phalanx. Fans of the visiting team are bused, walked inside a line formed by policemen with helmets and shields, and are corralled in the stadium. Rival tribes are meant to be kept physically apart once inside under the forceful supervision of the police, and this separation requires meticulous planning.

During the game, the hooligans will delineate their space through sounds, songs, and the waving of flags in the light of flares and rock to their own rhythm. The tone will be threatening, and the words insulting to the other team, its players, and supporters. The intent is to intimidate the other brigade or firm and make the opponents on the field lose their concentration. The hooligan fans become actors in the match being played.

The singing and shouting is often purposefully racist, an increasing trend in Europe. Soccer stadiums have become arenas where racism can be openly expressed. Some firms and brigades claim to have or do have real affiliations with rightwing political groups, whose ideologies are particularly attractive to young fans seeking strong identification. Spain now holds a prominent spot in the list of countries where racist incidents take place.

Outside the stadium, before and after the game, "firms" will provoke, scare, and beat rivals and occasionally uninvolved passersby. It is wise for spectators to be knowledgeable about their idiosyncrasies. Walking out of White Hart Lane (home to Tottenham soccer club) wearing a red shirt (the color of Arsenal) after a Tottenham-Arsenal game is looking for trouble, as my son Nicholas once discovered.

He went to the game with his friend J.T. Arsenal won. The Tottenham "Spurs" fans exited the stadium looking for revenge. Nick walked ahead of J.T, the red of his Arsenal shirt poorly hidden under his jacket. A group of seven or eight Spurs spotted him. He was an easy target despite the dense police presence. The tactics of the hooligans were well known: bump and jostle Nick into an alley and beat him to a pulp. But J.T jumped into the fray, waved his credentials as a true American Tottenham fan, stunned the group with his knowledge about the game, played Judas to his friend by denouncing his stupidity and acted so convincingly that the two friends escaped unscathed.

Violent incidents after the game are always feared. Few visiting hooligans can avoid the projectiles that will rain on them, and none of their buses will be left undented. This sad routine becomes a tragedy on certain occasions.

Hooliganism is at its worst when groups of fans travel to the site of international competitions. All the elements of a destructive mixture are there, the renewal of bonds with like-minded peers while traveling, the heavy drinking on the eve and day of the game, the dehumanization of people of other nationalities, the pride of being an Englishman outsmarting the local police or of being a member of the Italian police crushing the bodies of English fans etc… (Note 18). The scenario is even more dramatic when national teams are involved. The honor of the club is replaced by the pride of the nation, of being English or Italian or any of a number of nationalities.

Western societies have wagered that an extensive set of appropriate rules should allow people to live in communities while retaining their individuality. On one hand, institutions and laws are meant to protect freedom of expression, civil liberties, private property, etc… On the other, individuals accept to surrender the protection of these rights to groups of their peers. They entrust their legal rights, their physical safety, and the safeguard of the goods they own to the judiciary, law enforcement, and the army (Note 19). Society extends this protection to all its members. Underlying this quid pro quo is the understanding that groups of people cannot claim that they are exempted. Parents cannot physically harm their children nor can groups of fans agree that they will kill each other's members. That is not to say that some people in some parts of a country will not consider that the institutions are not fulfilling their duties and take over their own protection by becoming vigilantes, but this must remain an exception to the norm. Rampaging and causing physical or mental pain to others defies the rules which protect members of a society. When people set their sight on a sport event, say, a soccer game in Paris, Rome or London, meet before the event and spend the rest of the day indiscriminately causing serious physical harm and destroying property, they are attacking the very fiber of their own society. The question that has been asked again and again is why this destructive behavior?

In their vast majority hooligans are young people and are already considered old when they are in their thirties. Their behavior has been tied to their search for belonging, not only being part of a group but being seen as being part of that group. Using violence attracts attention, affirms their existence, and gives them an identity. Hooligans have also been seen as people with poorly formed identities, who have not been taught how to exercise self-control, whose environment condones violence. This has led over the years to "politically incorrect" assertions that they are associated mainly with lower classes.

Hooligans belong to tribes which provide protection to those who want to be abusive. Heavy consumption of alcohol, a must at any of their gatherings, is a further cause of low levels of self-control. Some are members of groups bent on changing society, usually extreme right movements which call for violence to protect the "white race."

In Europe, hooligans commit their exactions mostly in and around soccer stadiums. They rationalize their behavior by proclaiming their love of the game and of their team. This raises the question: are sports events a convenient forum to exhibit asocial behavior, or is aggressivity a by product of sport fandom?

SPORT CROWDS AND VIOLENCE

Sports events taking place in stadiums are an ideal venue for "firms." The time and place of games are known and allow for the preparation of gatherings and "actions." Anyone wanting to publicize a cause will find that such events offer opportunities for large public exposure and ample media coverage. Crowds are a convenient cover to any form of reprehensible behavior since they offer a mask behind which those bent on perpetuating uncivil acts can hide.

It is also true that, as Orwell wrote, "Sport…is war minus the shooting."

The causal relationship between sport and aggression has been extensively researched by academics. There are two major views: one that sport is a suitable outlet for violent instincts, and the other that witnessing sport competitions renders fans aggressive (Note 20).

The first theory has led to the popular creed that sport is a place for "blowing off steam." Its champion, historically, has been Konrad Lorenz who in *On Aggression,* written in 1963, asserted that aggression is a spontaneous drive which results from a buildup of energy. This energy will explode in violence if not discharged by aggressive behavior or diverted to ritualized activities like sport. Today's civilized man suffers from the lack of sufficient outlets for his accumulated energy. In order to lessen the risk of violence, he needs suitable diversions such as athletic competitions. The level of violence in a group would thus be reduced when its members participate as actors or spectators in sport events. This view is similar to the catharsis hypothesis, which claims that the display of competitive behavior in fantasy, play, or real life will reduce the aggressive urge. These energy-driven approaches are favored by ethologists who believe in the predominance of instinct in human behavior.

Lorenz's views appealed to the general public but have been seriously questioned by social psychologists who believe in the importance of learning and environmental stimuli. They claim that, even if pent-up energy is discharged in competitive sport, it does not lead to a reduction in aggressive drives. Aggression most likely leads to more aggression. They observe that the context of sport competitions increases the potential for belligerent behavior since these events are a source of excessive excitement. They sometimes mimic "war games," are often witnessed by large crowds, which tend to exacerbate the reactions of individuals, and are the occasion for unreasonable consumption of alcohol.

People who become aggressive at and around sports events are attracted by violence. This assumption finds support in the numerous books written by hooligans. Dougie Brimson, among others, refers repeatedly to the pleasure found in physical violence (Note 21).

It cannot be denied that sport competitions, say soccer games in large stadiums located in urban areas, offer favorable conditions to planning violent actions. There is also merit to the argument that these competitions can foster aggressive behavior. But sociologists believe that this is not the cause of hooligan behavior. Their behavior is the product of their personal history and social environment; sport is mostly a convenient catalyst.

Anecdotal evidence in support of this view that hooliganism is not a consequence of sport fandom per se can be found in a comparison between soccer, rugby, and American football. These three sports have close historical ties, and by design, rugby and football require a greater degree of physical contact. Nevertheless, as is well known in Europe, crowds at rugby games rarely exhibit the violent behavior of their peers at soccer games and, as discussed at the end of this chapter, hooliganism has not contaminated football in America.

All the factors that contribute to an understanding of the behavior of hooligans still do not explain why violence can spread like a bushfire at any one of these soccer venues and become so intense. Couldn't the same conditions, the theatricalization of violence, the heralding of extreme causes lead to less destructive forms of behavior?

The search for an answer led an American journalist to join English hooligans in the 80's. He became one of them and in a book titled *Among the Thugs* related his hair-raising experiences. Bill Buford was beaten "not as a human being but as some kind of object" by Italian police in Sardinia on the day England was facing Holland during Italia '90. In another context, he rubbed elbows with the rank and file of the National Front at a pub party, where skinheads ended up the evening in a trance and, as he writes,

"I am still not sure what happened between Dougie's swinging a chair over his head and Dougie's pinning me against a lamppost."

He had been curious about the fascist group whose racist songs can be heard at soccer games and who are known to make deliberate efforts to recruit soccer fans.

During his quest to understand why young English males were rioting, Buford was told about the highs of creating fear and hurting people, how it gives the same transcending experience as being on drugs. He himself felt these elemental pleasures and was fascinated by crowd violence. While amidst such crowds, he became aware of the eeriness before the carnage starts, before ordinary people move to another universe and throw away any acknowledgement of what they owe to society, excited by crossing the line into the antisocial. People forming a crowd, held back by what makes them civilized, suddenly endorse another personality. What triggers the crossing of thresholds? What makes members of a group walking down a street outside of a stadium start barbarously beating passersby, destroying cars, and vandalizing stores? Buford could not find legitimate causes to organized violence particularly crowd violence. It might be as desperately simple as "because they have nothing else to do."

When they have exhausted their antisocial kick, the thugs go home and behave like ordinary fathers or take their wife to the local pub, an extraordinary transformation, which confirms that they abandon all sense of individual responsibility when they join a hooligan tribe.

I did not duplicate Bill Buford's experience and mingled with PSG hooligans to dissect the why of organized crowd violence. I do, though, relate to his description of the moment in time when people are ready to throw out the rules of civil society and recede into a primitive state. It reminds me of dog fights. I walk my two male dogs on the same fields most days and let them roam. From time to time, they will spot other dogs, and when these are newcomers, particularly males, I have to stay alert. They will approach these other dogs, fur raised on their backs, and the standoff begins. They will freeze and, after a moment which always seems long, the balance between their training and their instincts will shift, and their attitude will change. On lucky days, they run to me or become playful; on others, they start a ferocious sounding fight. Over time, I have reduced the number of cases where the stand-off has shifted to aggression. Promising a treat, keeping my voice calm, maintaining a physical behavior familiar to them, all has helped, but I am not immune to the unexpected spark, the movement or noise that will trigger a fight. I will borrow a page from the writings of ethologists and draw an analogy between the behavior of my dogs and that of hooligans. Both succumb to aggressivity when instincts overpower learned behavior.

Increasing the presence of police, making the stadiums "all seaters" (no standing areas), tracking the worst offenders, addressing the needs of fan groups, calling on their civic obligations, etc... are measures aimed at changing the balance between nature and nurture. They have helped contain the problem, particularly in England. But society is still at the mercy of explosions of violence by hooligans because too many sparks can cause them to shift into incivility and even crime. There will always be young males, admirers of physical toughness, joining crowds at soccer stadiums in the hope that one more time their tribe will allow them for a while to become someone else and find pleasure in being dangerous for anyone they don't consider their peer.

Too many men succumb too easily to the highs of violence. In whatever society they live, they grab justifications to inflict physical pain on others. Every year on Good Friday, I hear the Passion of Jesus Christ, a story of physical pain. I read about a little known moment in history, the inhuman treatment of Kikuyus in Kenya after the Mau Mau rebellion, page upon page of torture by supposedly civilized representatives of Her Majesty, and I recently watched on PBS one more history of the KKK, of white males out in the dark of night trying to get themselves a nigger. The debates about this element of human nature are mostly between the followers of Thomas Hobbes, who contend that violent instincts are restrained by social conditioning, and those of Jean Jacques Rousseau, who see men corrupted by society. Those who search for an answer in the evolution of men find more and more support for the theories of the 17th century English philosopher. As Ian Parker wrote in an article on bonobos in The New Yorker's July, 30 2007 edition, it is possible to see "a clear line of thuggery from ape ancestry to human prehistory and on to Srebrenica."

Hooligans use a weak cause, their attachment to a soccer club, and a forum, the soccer stadium, to inflict violence. Society, led by management of clubs and local authorities, is constantly fighting this plague. It has won many battles but not the war. Laws have been passed specifically to fight violence at sport events. Sozialarbeiters (Social workers) have been used in Germany to facilitate the integration of these fans in the local community. Alain Cayzac, acknowledging the enormous part that this problem played in the life of his club, listed some of the measures taken during the years preceding our meeting in September 2005. PSG organized information campaigns to help fight racism. Its managers listened to the specific demands of the hooligan fan groups. They understood that they want to be acknowledged, want a say in the management, and consider certain areas of the stadiums to be their domain. The club built strategies accordingly, negotiated with these Fan Clubs, and entered into agreements which define the rights and duties of both parties. Unfortunately, during the subsequent seasons, PSG was still involved in too many incidents.

HOOLIGANS IN THE U.S?

All of this is rather foreign to American fans more used to excessive rowdiness than to planned violence. They are familiar with the "Carnival" environment and rarely face cases of organized asocial behavior. Hooliganism, i.e., acts of premeditated aggressions at and around sports events, has not taken root in the U.S. The numerous tribes of young adults seeking recognition through the use of violence join gangs.

Gangs can be traced to the first major waves of immigrants and can be found throughout the U.S. (Note 22). The Department of Justice published a report in April 2001 entitled *The Growth of Youth Gang Problems in the U.S., 1970–1998*. It analyzes their dramatic growth in number and geographical distribution and traces it to several interacting influences, including the historic immigrant gang tradition, the increase in female headed households, the "branching out" of formerly localized groups and most importantly drugs. Today's gangs are a far cry from the "Jets "and "Sharks" romanticized in *West Side Story*.

They are not active at or around sports competitions in the U.S. The atmosphere surrounding such events is meant to be festive. Some fans might look scary, but most are harmless. To be sure, there can be high levels of rowdiness, mostly due to drunkenness. No venue or sport is immune. A fight broke out between players and spectators in Detroit at the end of a Piston-Pacers basketball game in November 2004. The out of control, vulgar, and violent behavior of fans at professional football games is well documented and has been vividly described by Dennis Perrin in his book *American Fan*; it could be argued that the fans of the Philadelphia Eagles, the football team that I support against my better judgment, have the worst reputation. In its March 3rd 2008 issue, *Sports Illustrated* reported on the extreme vulgarity and taunting by college basketball fans and asked, "How much is too much?" Unfortunately, reprehensible behavior starts in high school. A hockey game on March 1st 2008 between Darien and New Canaan High Schools in Fairfield County, whose students swell the ranks of Ivy League Freshman classes, ended in a near riot with eight boys being arrested. Much of this is reminiscent of many a soccer game in Europe and raises similar questions about why? and what to do? But violence at sports events in the U.S is not planned and endemic in football, basketball, or even hockey. It cannot be called hooliganism.

Why don't American fans form English type "firms" or Italian type "brigades"? Why don't gangs fight for recognition in and around stadiums in the U.S.? Many reasons are given, which refer to the geography and history of the country, the lesser level of sectarianism and of loyalty towards professional sports teams. These arguments need to be viewed in the light of how "hooligan tribes" came into existence in the UK.

Violence has always been associated with games and then with sports; it became a regular feature of English soccer in the second half of the 20th century. The terrain was ideal for the waging of wars between tribes of fans: the stadiums were in the center of cities, the "curves" had no seats, and the competing teams were coming from around the corner. The battlefield was in the streets and in the open spaces inside the stadium, the assembling of the troops facilitated by the short distances separating the home turf of most firms. In London itself, there were and still are up to six teams competing in the top soccer league. A similar description could be made of the Italian scene with rivalries between towns going back centuries and the publicizing of extremist political ideas by groups of fans, an aggravating factor.

It does not seem that any specific event marked the birth of hooliganism in English soccer. Presumably, favorable conditions reached a critical mass: fans of local and visiting teams making the curves of stadiums their territory, words of songs becoming more insulting, incidents between groups of fans leading to desire for revenge. Slowly, memories were built, reputations needed to be defended, and this led to a cycle of acts of violence still alive in the 21st century. The story of this or that famous fight involving the supporters of West Ham or Chelsea or of any other English soccer team resembles the accounts of battles before the invention of fire arms: men, unafraid of physical harm, leading their troops to the conquest and occupation of territories and long-standing rivalries between clans.

Similar conditions are not found in the U.S. Sport fandom starts at the high school and college level, and the world of professional sport is a separate one. Games taking place in educational institutions are not conducive to repeated and planned demonstrations of physical violence. There are occasional bursts of vulgarity and violence. There are numerous rivalries. American football fields are the forums of many intense ones; yearly gatherings mimic ancient battles. The Ohio State Buckeyes against the Michigan Wolverines is a ritual taking place in modern coliseums, pitting legendary coaches against each other. The Washington Massillon Tigers facing the Canton Mc Kinley Bulldogs are do-or-die affairs for the senior players and confrontations whose memories feed endless conversations in these two Ohio communities. Yale-Harvard is the enactment of a long tradition, reminiscent of the very first sports events that took place on English college grounds. The Game, as it is called, is dated back to 1875 when football was still a version of rugby and soccer. The outcomes of these battles do matter for students, alumnae, and local communities; it is a yearly test of their identity; but they are not tragic affairs. They generate a high level of excitement and tension with an acceptable dose of rowdiness.

There are also "local" rivalries between professional teams in the most popular sports, but few have a history of violence. They are mostly about bragging rights. The physical context is not favorable to the waging of wars: the supporters from the visiting teams come from towns located far away, the logistics of assembling troops is daunting, the stadiums are mainly outside of urban areas, and there is no history of bloodshed. Above all, professional sport has been a business in the U.S. for a long time and now belongs with the entertainment industry. Stadiums are not places that one chooses to settle scores but where one goes to have fun. The parking lots around stadiums are for tailgating, not wielding knifes.

Sport fits the model of American society, which is said to offer anyone a chance to succeed and, more importantly, a second chance. If your business goes bankrupt, try again and hope for better luck; society will not think less of you because you failed the first time. There is hope, the guiding force of a young nation, the belief that hard work with a dose of luck will allow one to reach his dream.

The same spirit is meant to guide sports teams and athletes: draw lessons from today's loss and get ready for the next game; there is always another competition to win.

Americans view sport as a land of many opportunities. They love it, and it is part of their culture.

⸻ ⸻ ⸻

NOTE 15

Warren St. John makes extensive references to Le Bon in a chapter called "The Era of Crowds" in *Rammer, Jammer, Yellow Hammer,* and Bill Buford does likewise in his book *Among the Thugs.*

An article in *The Financial Times* dated September 5, 2005 and entitled "The Quest for Mastery of the Madding Crowd" talks about crowds' reputation for being dangerous entities and how these beliefs have remained essentially unchanged since Gustave Le Bon "…declared more than a century ago that crowds are little more than madhouses on legs." The article, in fact, is about a theory put forth by certain experts that the behavior of crowds during "stampede" and "mass panic" is predictable.

NOTE 16

The elements of the social identity theory listed here are detailed in papers published under the direction of Serge Moscovici, director at the Graduate School of Social Sciences in Paris.

NOTE 17

Uncontrolled expression of emotions is not accepted at all sport events. Some, such as tennis, used to require the same type of behavior from their spectators as classical music concerts: respect for the performers and release of feelings only at prescribed moments. This similitude can be traced to the history of both activities. As tennis became more popular, the behavior of spectators became rowdier.

NOTE 18

One example: in 2007, the police in Rome showed too much muscle and sent quite a few Manchester United fans to the hospital.

NOTE 19

As a point of reference, Greek cities did not have public institutions to protect the law. Each citizen was entrusted with the responsibility to denounce to the magistrates those who were breaking the law. There were also professional public denunciators, the so-called sycophants.

NOTE 20

Leonard Berkowitz, who used to teach at the Department of Psychology, University of Madison-Wisconsin, and is well known for his studies on human aggression, published an article in the "American Scientist" in 1969, titled *Simple views on Aggression*. I have relied on his "simple views" for my references to the relevant theories.

NOTE 21

Dougie Brimson's *Everywhere We Go* was published in 1996, and *Barmy Army* in 2000.

NOTE 22

The fights involving Irish immigrants trying to carve a place for themselves in the 19th century are vividly portrayed in the movie *Gangs of New York*.

REFLECTIONS ON FANATICS

I started this book with the theory that a similar road leads to fandom and fanaticism and have focused up to now on sports fans.

The "anatomy of sports fans" confirms that these fans have much in common with other forms of fanaticism.

The final chapter examines these other manifestations of fanaticism and, more particularly, the darker ones.

CHAPTER 8

"There is no telling to what extremes of cruelty and ruthlessness a man will go when he is freed from the fears, hesitations, doubt and the vague stirrings of decency that go with individual judgment."
<u>The True Believer</u> by Eric Hoffer.

Men in search of an identity, a sense of recognition, of belonging, who join tribes or causes become fanatics when they invest conspicuous amounts of energy in defending their choice. This is a defining feature of fanaticism and is expressed in physical excitement, in striving for perfection or in blind passion unhindered by doubt.

Fanaticism is characterized as much by form as by substance. The substance, in other words, the cause, seems to be secondary. It is the intensity of his behavior which sets the fanatic apart from other men. Using the phenomenological approach developed by Joseph Rudin in *Fanaticism,* written in 1965, one can include in the world of fanatics the overly enthusiastic sports fan, the passionate anthropologist, and the monomaniacal, unscrupulous revolutionary.

The word "fanatic" comes from "fanum," which means "temple" in Latin, the sacred place where the oracles were pronounced. The fanatici had knowledge, while access to the temple was forbidden to the profane.

In 18th century England, the fanatics were called enthusiasts. They believed themselves to be possessed by a God but were considered by others to be false prophets. It was a period when a Robert Ross, Pastor (1726–1790) wrote an opus titled *Plain address to the Quakers, Moravians, Separatists, Separate-Baptists, Rogerenes and other **enthusiasts**; on immediate impulses and revelations.* Since the Enlightment, intransigent adherents to religious and ideological movements are called fanatics and also known as "true believers."

THE ENTHUSIAST AND THE PASSIONATE

The most benign form of fanatical behavior is excitement for the sake of excitement. People exhibiting such behavior are referred to as enthusiasts, not with the etymological meaning previously mentioned but with today's understanding of exuberant. They are excessive in the physical manifestation of their emotions. The object of such emotions is irrelevant, the experience is the reward in itself. Enthusiasts feel free to share their excitement when they are part of a crowd. They can be seen at rock concerts or among those trying to catch a glimpse of a movie star. Gathered in a stadium, they are the excited but mostly harmless sport fans.

Manifestations of enthusiasm are frowned upon in today's society; even the best of news is no excuse for noisy acknowledgment and infringing the space of others. It is worth going back to the historical developments, mentioned in Chapter 5 that led to these restraints. During his "civilizing process" man became conscious of his self versus others and ashamed and repelled by bodily functions. The soul-body dualism, "the two components of a divided self," as Augustine wrote, became mind-body after the Enlightment. This led to the mind wanting to control the body. Society put a lid on the physical manifestation of excitement in public, and this resulted in the "Victorian man" of 19th century England, who believed in self-control and self-restraint. He lived in "the age of cant," which Byron judged so severely; cant because the Victorian virtues were imposing unnatural restraints on emotions. Western society still lives in the shadow of the Victorian man. Being well-mannered is synonymous with showing physical restraint.

We know that these rules do not apply to the behavior of the average sport fan in a stadium because society has accepted that men participating in certain leisure activities can be "uncivilized."

Passionate people, also, exhibit fanatic intensity in their behavior. Josef Rudin writes,

"While the intensity of excitement does not necessarily imply fanatic traits, it seems that a great passion is hardly thinkable without a touch of fanatic tendency."

The New York Times and *"60 Minutes"* reported during the summer of 2005 on those bird lovers dedicated to sighting an Ivory Billed Woodpecker in the swamps of Arkansas. It is for these people a lifelong pursuit to prove to the world of ornithologists that the bird has not disappeared. As the article said, in the church of birds, passions run high. It stopped just short of referring to them as fanatics. *The Wall Street Journal* did use the "f "word when in June 2005, it published an article on Hank Greenberg. Describing his obsessive tracking of the stock price of AIG when he was its Chairman (American International Group, the insurance group which made the headlines of the financial papers in September 2008) the Journal noted that "(his) interests were perfectly-even *fanatically*- aligned with those of his shareholders."

If some men did not devote their lives to new ideas and adventures, nothing would be achieved.

The explorers of the South Pole exemplify intense devotion to a pursuit. Roald Amundsen's dash, Robert Falcon Scott's ill-fated expedition, and Ernest Shackleton's survival epic, all exhibit the endurance and one-track mind of men driven by a goal. They were, without a doubt, fanatics, but with their peers who climbed Mount Everest, circumnavigated the globe, went deeper into the oceans and further in space, they enlarged the circle of human knowledge and extended the limits of man's achievements. Great athletes in the pursuit of a record exhibit a similar high degree of passion in their physical and mental toughness.

The passions driving men searching for new horizons are the bane of men of reason. The late Robert C. Solomon, who taught philosophy at the University of Texas, wrote that passions have always been treated as inferior and disruptive forces. Actually, whenever in politics or business a group presents new ideas with passion, those who prefer the status quo will say, "Let's be reasonable." They are hiding behind the argument that emotions can be disruptive in an attempt to protect their turf.

Because man can be overpowered by his passions, the question of how he should deal with them has been addressed since the Greek philosophers. The Stoics favored apathy (etymologically, absence of emotions). Actually, it was not absence of emotions that they recommended; it was, as reported by a contributor to Wikipedia, "to avoid emotional troubles by developing clear judgment and inner calm through diligent practice of logic, reflection and concentration." In the 18th century, a British philosopher, the 3rd Earl of Shaftesbury, brought a new dimension to stoicism by stressing the pitfalls not only of passion but also of excessive reason. In *A Letter concerning Enthusiasm,* published in 1708, he writes that enthusiasm is the spirit "which allotted the heroes, statesmen, poets etc" but that it can become "extravagance and fury" (read: fanaticism) so it needs to be controlled. This much had been said before him, but he offered a novel approach to avoid the pitfalls of fanaticism: wit and good sense. Stay skeptical, avoid pretentious gravity ("gravity is the very essence of imposture"), and give liberty to wit.

Long before Lord Shaftesbury, Aristotle had championed the concept of the "golden mean," the mean between extremes, to guide man in his actions. In Book IV of his *Ethics,* he considered the disciplining of passions as high virtue He did not have negative views on passions; what matters is which techniques we develop to deal with them. Man should not be judged by the feelings he has but by what he does with his emotions and passions. He should not become a slave to passions and should control them by reason, find through habit what amount of emotion will give him pleasure. If Aristotle were alive today, he might observe that there is nothing wrong with being an exuberant sport fan as long as the fan learns to control his passion and understands that pleasure needs to be disciplined.

In *The Passions,* Robert C Solomon defended the theory that emotions are intelligent, they are man's way to be tuned to the world; our passions define who we are and the world we live in. Of course, as Solomon wrote, not all passions are life-enhancing. "All emotions make life meaningful, but some meanings are demeaning." And then, even though passions can be viewed as the energy that drives the self, they can make others feel uncomfortable. This side of man can get out of control, and he can be perceived as too disruptive to his social environment. It is particularly true when he invests large amounts of energy in defending ideas which go against the creeds of society at that point in time. The biographies of two men who let themselves be driven by their beliefs while their ideas were rejected by the establishment can be found in "Appendix 1." One is Eugene Dubois, the other Galileo.

Galileo Galilei (1564–1642) was passionate about astronomy. He became a believer of heliocentrism, the concept that earth revolves around the sun, at a time when the Holy Office in Rome interpreted the scriptures to say that the sun traveled around the earth. Nicolas Copernicus had presented the heliocentric assumption in *De revolutionibus orbum coelestium* published in 1543 shortly before his death, and in 1616, the Catholic Church had banned Copernicus's work. Galileo was well aware that presenting heliocentrism as anything other than a mathematical model would enrage Rome. He was too passionate about his beliefs, though, and did publish in 1632 a book known as *Dialogues,* which was a poorly disguised defense of heliocentrism. The "establishment" could not allow such ideas to spread. The Catholic Church, threatened by Protestantism, could not afford to be lax on doctrine. The work was put on the "index" of forbidden books, and Galileo was accused by the Inquisition of heresy. He had defended a scientific position which would prove to be true but was silenced because it went against the orthodoxy of the time.

Eugene Dubois went one step further. His passion, uncontrolled by reason, led to real fanaticism. Born in Holland in 1858, a year before Darwin published *The Origin of Species,* he became an early evolutionist. This was the first step of what would become the lifelong pursuit of the discovery of fossils of the so-called "missing link" between apes and men. His studies of paleontology, geology, and natural history led him to look for this missing link in Sumatra and then Java.

This was an extraordinary venture. After five years of stubborn searching, he found an apelike skull and a humanlike femur, which he claimed had belonged to the same animal. He called it "Pithecanthropus Erectus." His discovery met with a lot of skepticism. He had expected the resistance of the scientific world, the more so because anything having to do with human evolution was controversial, but he could not allow his success to be ignored. Having invested so much energy in his search, he became more and more protective of his discovery. From a man driven by a passion he became a real fanatic, obsessive, rigid, and intolerant. He died in solitude in 1940.

A fine line separates these men, the passionate explorers and those fighting the sclerosis of entrenched human beliefs from real fanatics. Gitta Sereny, who wrote several illuminating books on Hitler's Germany, tells a story which illustrates this point. Born in 1923 to a Protestant family and having lost her father, an Anglophile Hungarian, when she was two, she attended boarding school in England and returned to Vienna when she was fourteen.

In *The German Trauma*, she describes her experience as an eleven year old schoolgirl on her way to England, witnessing a Nazi Party Congress in Nuremberg in 1934:

"I was overcome by the symmetry of the marchers, many of them children like me; the joyful faces all around; the rhythm of the sounds; the solemnity of the silences; the colors of the flags; the magic of the lights. One moment I was enraptured, glued to my seat; the next, I was standing up, shouting with joy along with thousands of others. I saw the men on the distant podium and heard their hugely amplified voices. But I understood nothing; it was the drama, the theater of it all that overwhelmed me."

In March 1938, Hitler invaded Austria, and she heard for the first time, a rhythmic chant that echoed around Vienna for weeks, "Germany awake, Jewry perish," and even though she became aware of the injustice and cruelty in her world, when she heard Hitler speak, she felt excited.

"What was it in him that drew us? What was it in us-in me too that day-that allowed ourselves to be drawn?"

A few months later, her mother had to leave Vienna precipitously, and they both settled in Switzerland. The spell was broken. She ended up working for the Allies during and after the war.

For a moment in her life, she had been caught by "the theater of it all." What would it have taken to go to the next step and lose herself in the cause? Her background, education, and sensibility did not predispose her to join the Hitler Jugend, but for Gitta, how many other enthusiasts became true fanatics?

THE REAL FANATICS

"The less justified a man is in claiming excellence for his own self, the more ready he is to claim excellence for his nation, his race or his holy cause."

This quote is from *The True Believer* (1951) by Eric Hoffer, a brilliant and insightful introduction to real fanatics. Hoffer was a self-educated longshoreman. At the age of eighteen, he had moved from the Bronx to the West Coast, supporting himself with odd jobs and seeking education in the public libraries of California. He later joined the Longshoreman Union but always continued his self-education. His main focus in *The True Believer* is on mass movements and on the motivations of men who endorse a cause. His working hypothesis is that "the frustrated predominate among the early adherents of all mass movements" and that the active phase of these movements is dominated by the true believer, the man of fanatic faith. He develops the fundamental theme that fanatics are searching for something that they do not find in themselves. What matters when they join a cause is not what that specific cause represents but that they cease to be themselves and become part of something which gives them hope. His thinking was colored by the events in Europe of the 30's and 40's; his insights, though, are applicable to men joining any manner of group. Even though much could be referenced, only a few quotes have been scattered throughout this chapter (indicated by italics and marked *E.H.*). Eric Hoffer was truly an exceptional man who produced a seminal work. His "true believers" are the instruments of the bad things done in the name of religious, social, and political movements. They are of all times because man's urge to represent something absolute seems ineradicable.

Real fanatics are men who believe that their faith has led them to absolute truths, who do not question these truths, and expend excessive amounts of energy defending their beliefs.

What is faith in the context of the above definition? It is, paraphrasing what Anthony Kenny wrote in *Faith and Reason*, the way to truths which would otherwise be beyond the reach of the mind. When man cannot find in his world answers to his questions, he calls upon faith to enlighten his reason. Faith can be unreasonable, but who is to decide? People can refuse to examine evidence, which might lead them to revise beliefs that they have acquired through faith. This is what true fanatics do. This relationship between faith and reason is at the core of fanaticism.

What are the questions answered by faith? Men have always needed to understand how they relate to the universe and felt the urge to give meaning to their lifes. When their mind could not find in the world the answers to predicaments they have imagined other realities and believed in the existence of absolute truths. Man also needs benchmarks to guide him during his life on earth. The more he lives in the company of others, the more he needs to know what they expect from him and what he can expect from them. Causes will offer him answers in his search for an understanding of his relationship to the universe, his fellow man and to himself. He will be led by faith to believe that there are truths, which will give him hope and guidance.

Religions and ideologies have played a prominent role in the history of fanaticism. In the search for answers to questions that defy reason, humankind seems to have an inherent drive to believe in something transcendent, in "hope beyond reason" as the anthropologist Scott Atran calls it. Religions that share certain supernatural features are found in virtually every culture, and Darwinian scientists tend to agree that religious belief is an outgrowth of brain architecture even if they disagree about whether belief itself was adaptive or an evolutionary byproduct.

It can be reasonably assumed from the study of later cultures and people such as the Australian aborigines that hunters in the Paleolithic period lived with fears and anxieties, that they had questions that they could not answer, and that to help them go through their day-to-day lives they imagined other realities peopled with spirits and deities. Karen Armstrong writes in A *Short History of Myth* that they must have conceived myths and observed rituals. There was no separation in their world between the sacred and the profane. The other realities that they conceived touched their lives. Their imagination was the road that led them to the truths that helped them survive.

Much later in history, religions and philosophical systems evolved in India (Hinduism, Buddhism) and China that also imagined other realities, but these had fewer resemblances with the real world and were peopled with deities that were often less anthropomorphic. In the West, the Greek philosophers used rational discourse to try and understand how man relates to himself, to others, and to the world, but they, Plato and others, had to recognize that logic could go only so far in assuaging man's thirst for understanding and that some matters were the domain of the irrational. The Yahweh of the Israelites, which would become the only god of two more monotheisms, Christianity and Islam, replaced, mostly in the Middle East and the West, the deities and myths. Members of all three religions use faith to believe in stories that have been revealed to man; the Testaments and the Koran tell man how he has been created, what is expected of him, and have a similar eschatology.

Ideologies need faith to lead people to believe in absolute truths. These truths are utopias, ideal societies. They are conceived in man's mind, but masses cannot be convinced by reason alone. During the early stages of any movement, when eggs need to be broken before the omelet can be made, faith is called upon to keep people on the path to an idealized future. New ideologies are given all the appearances of religions through myths, ceremonies, and language. Two hold a prominent place in the recent history of fanaticism.

The French revolution started with the taking of the Bastille on July 14, 1789 and ended on November 9, 1799 when Napoleon Bonaparte staged a coup which installed a Consulate, a short but very intense period of history and a major landmark in Western Europe. Its roots go back to the Enlightenment, and its stated purpose was to free men from any bondage; reason would triumph over superstition and privilege. A new society was the answer to man's urge to believe in something. But vast and rapid change could not be realized without passion and true belief. By the end of 1793, reason was worshiped, and the "supreme being" was celebrated during carefully scripted ceremonies in June 1794 in Paris. Faith had replaced politics.

Germany was under the spell of Nazism from early 1933 to the spring of 1945. The movement had its roots in the country's defeat in 1918, which the German people were unable to accept; in the eyes of many, the army had been betrayed by the home front. Hitler and the party that he shaped, the National Socialist party, i.e. Nazi, used this frustration in their march to power. The utopia of Nazism was a united Volk, a superior race, and increased Lebensraum (space for Germany to expand). Hitler had carefully crafted an aura of infallibility and was the messiah of this political religion.

During these short periods in history, masses of people in France and Germany adopted these creeds, which promised better societies. Few had the lucidity or found the courage to question the causes that they were led to endorse. Most found comfort of being part of something and blindly followed commandments which told them what is right and what is wrong.

"The masses do not crave freedom of conscience but blind faith, authoritarian faith."E.H.

People find the absence of benchmarks unsettling. In *The Brothers Karamazov*, Ivan, one of the three brothers, recalls a poem he has written, an allegory about a pseudo-Second

Coming in Spain at the time of the Inquisition. The Inquisitor puts the man, Him, in prison, and Dostoyevsky writes:

"The Church has vanquished freedom and done so to make man happy because nothing has ever been more insupportable for a man and a human society than freedom."

That man is most at ease when he is given firm rules and goals explains the power of mass movements. It is well-documented that these remain strong only as long as their leaders are unwavering in the defense of their tenets. The examples often given are the rise of Protestantism as a reaction against the laxity of the Catholic Church and the fall of Communism caused by the party becoming soft on liberal ideals.

"...the effectiveness of a doctrine should not be judged by its profundity, sublimity or the validity of the truths it embodies, but by how thoroughly it insulates the individual from his self and the world as it is." E.H.

Men who have reached truths which guide them through their lives have entered a box. What matters is not what is in it, which religion, ideology, nation etc., but that it makes them feel secure and, most importantly, it gives them hope. It can be the promise of a brighter future, an afterlife in a paradise, a better karma, power, and glory at the end of a long struggle. They need to believe that what is in the box has a promise, however long and difficult the road before they get rewarded. In that sense, they are similar to the men who passionately believe in an idea and make huge sacrifices to reach their goals, to get to the South Pole or find the missing link.

What the believer finds in the box becomes his reality, and he adopts its certitudes. The rules are known, and he is protected by the shadows of those other humans who share the same beliefs. He is the heir of prehistoric men who imagined other realities to conquer their fears.

Having found hope and security, men led by faith can identify and be identified with something bigger than themselves.

Most humans who are in some box are there because of their background and environment. They tend to stay where their history has put them. Sociological studies in the U.S and Western Europe show that the majority of people have the religion into which they were born. In his novel *The Plot against America,* Philip Roth captures this notion in a few words. Describing why Jews living in New Jersey during the Second World War were being Jews, he writes:

> "What they were was what they couldn't get rid of – what they couldn't begin to want to get rid of....Their being Jews issued from their being themselves..."

The Catholic Church in the U.S. was built over time by the faithful coming from Europe and South America, and it still reflects, in its diversity, the national origin of each wave of immigrants; the Irish and Italian on the East Coast, the Hispanics in the Southwest, or the Poles in the Midwest.

The dynamics of unloading the weight of history and being born again are complex. A conversion from a religious, political, or any form of belief is disruptive for an individual and the people around him. When it takes place, social factors are predominant in the choice of the new belief and kinship, and friendship play a major role. The convert joins a new social group and then adopts new creeds.

Because the so-called born again feel empowered by the new truths that they endorse, they are candidates to becoming true fanatics. New ideas and causes need converts who are fully committed. If their supporters are wavering, they will not succeed in spreading their truths. It takes passion and faith to change society. Those who go against established values and beliefs will have fanatical tendencies by necessity and will be heretics by definition. Two thousand years ago, the Christians were heretics, and the Romans considered them to be fanatics. The Romans wanted their world to be orderly; the new religion was excessive and exclusive and a threat to their social order. Christianity was a "superstitio" before becoming a "religio" in the 3rd century. Two hundred years ago the adherents of new religious sects were called the enthusiasts, i.e. fanatics. In both cases, heretics were labeled fanatics. Throughout history, calling heretics fanatics has led to many a religious or ideological war. It is often overlooked that the defenders of orthodoxy also need to be unwavering in their commitment if they want to preserve the status quo; they also need to be fanatics.

Most people who have been led to truths by faith and do not question these truths know that not everyone shares their beliefs. They will consider that their mission is to spread the "good news" and do so while respecting their fellow humans.

Those that Eric Hoffer calls "true believers" do not.

True believers are men who believe that faith has led them to absolute truths, who do not question these truths and dehumanize those who do not share their beliefs.

The pride that they have in their creed turns into dangerous arrogance. The unconditional defenders of truths reached through faith, the defenders of myths or of warped realities (such as the deniers of the Holocaust) segregate, demonize, and eventually try to eliminate those who are not part of their flock, who are outside of their box. They have abandoned any reasonable consideration of what led them to their truth and of the sanctity of other human beings. They see the world as a struggle between good and evil, light opposed to darkness: I versus the other, my belief versus the beliefs of others. In order to fulfill their need for affirmation and power, the true believers will define others as "Untermenschen" (subhuman). These fanatics have use for only one half of the Manichean dualism. They do not acknowledge that tension between positive and negative can be enriching. They want to ignore, as Francois Jullien writes in *L'Ombre au Tableau*, that there are no shadows without light.

The process of dehumanizing others is simple to understand if not to justify. Whenever people are identified based on their race, nationality, creed, or other qualification and judged only by that label, the process has started. Those who look at the label feel justified to treat them as less worthy than themselves. As David O'Rourke relates in *Demons by Definition,* the Inquisitors used logic and cataloguing to justify the extermination of the Cathars, a religious sect present in the southwest of France in the 12th century. They would reason that the unity of society and its people was good, and any heresy which destroyed that unity was evil. The role of abstract definitions allowed single individuals to be lumped into classes of people. The use of class identification to catalog individuals would become a hallmark of the way dissent is treated in western society. People who ran death camps depersonalized their intended victims by defining them as members of an inferior class of humans.

How does a man of faith become a true believer? Scholars point to the psychological and sociological causes, the ties with unformed personal identities. Humans have basic needs such as a positive sense of self, a positive connection to others, a feeling of effectiveness. These are some of the essential building blocks of an identity, and they are the product of the personal and social history of an individual. When these needs are satisfied, people are capable of transcendence, which means to truly reach beyond themselves.

Most theologians, psychologists, and social scientists will say that absence of self-respect makes true love of others impossible. When people with an insufficient amount of self-esteem join a movement, they surrender their "self," they practice what is called "pseudo-transcendence," and this opens the door for them to become true believers (Note 23).

The text books also refer to the role played by frustration with one's environment. A sense of justice is an important basic human need. Those who feel frustrated by an unjust order of things will look for a cause to give them hope, and if they are incapable of true transcendence, they will surrender to that cause.

Self-sacrifice entices people to become dogmatic and blindly faithful. Obedience will have the better of their reason. They will slide down the same slope traveled by the participants in Milgram's experiment (Note 24) and progressively dehumanize those who do not belong to their cause.

People can seek the comfort of a cause to compensate for their frustrations and lack of self-esteem. When they believe that they have discovered truths which are absolute, that they do not question because they have been reached thanks to faith, they are on the road to becoming true believers. Enclosed in the box of their convictions, they are led to dehumanize those who do not share their beliefs. They move to the dark side of the world of fanatics.

Who were the fanatics who played a role in the cruelest phases of the French Revolution and were the instruments of Nazi terror? They were mostly frustrated members of the middle class. It was not the poor who needed to struggle daily to survive who peopled their ranks but those who had only gotten a taste of what they could have become. They are symbolized by the "intellectuel manqué" in France and "ordinary people" in Germany.

Both movements are known as mass movements, and throughout most of modern history it had been thought that mobs attract lower classes and people with a history of aggressivity and lawlessness. It was only in the latter part of the twentieth century that more specific research brought to light, as Robert A. Nye writes in *The Origins of Crowd Psychology* (1975), that "crowds are not simple aggregates of individuals out to loot and destroy in an irrational orgy." They are composed of people who bring their own anxieties and frustrations.

Before Nye, George Rude was the first historian to look at "the faces in the crowd," specifically during the French Revolution. In *The Crowd in History* (1964), he notes that vagrants and criminals played only a marginal role in the disturbances of 1789; the crowds were largely composed of sober householders and citizens admittedly of humble station. Rude surrounds these statements with a lot of caveats but has solid reasons to say that they are closer to reality than the traditional view. His attempt to present concisely what prompted people to take part encountered too much variety in motives and circumstances. What he notes, though, is that most certainly during the first years of the Revolution people rioted pushed by dire necessity as they had done numerous times before in Paris and in the French countryside; there was only one major "journee" in Paris where the price or supply of food or bread played no part. Popular disturbances after the beginning of the 90's took on another dimension as the "sans culottes" became indoctrinated with the new concepts of the "rights of man" and sovereignty of the people

(Note 25). Political and economic motivations became commingled, and "activist" participants added other faces to the crowds.

Then, in August 1792, the truly horrific phase of the Revolution began when the balance of power shifted from the elected Assembly towards the "Commune" of Paris. "Terror and Virtue" become the motto of those governing France, most visibly after September 1793 during the cruel days of the Terror. The members of the Commune were bourgeois, small business owners, or lawyers and were the first "terrorists," a word derived from the "terreur" that they fomented. To this day, it is difficult to understand what led mostly Parisian "petits bourgeois" to encourage massacres. Most certainly personal frustrations led them to join the anonymity of mass movements. The destructive obedience cited in connection with the Milgram experiment, the blind logic of partisanship, and other features of true fanaticism were also at play.

The true fanatics of Nazi Germany were the street brawlers of the paramilitary SA, the more disciplined SS led by Heinrich Himmler and the "Geheime Staatspolizei" (secret state police) known as Gestapo. Eric A. Johnson has done an exhaustive analysis of this last group in "*Nazi Terror: The Gestapo, Jews and Ordinary Germans*" published in 1999. He describes how the officers of the Gestapo were in large majority policemen who had learned their job during the Weimar Republic and very early on joined some of the National Socialist groups. Their reasons for joining match very closely the generic list presented earlier: unformed personalities, frustration, dissatisfaction with life, a need for a source of hope. They also had a more prosaic reason, opportunism, since the movement gave them a chance to advance their careers.

From the moment they joined, the die was cast. As one would expect from "true believers," they surrendered all judgment on the tenets of their cause and were totally devoted to it. The Gestapo gave them the values that guided their actions. Unconditionally committed to their professional responsibilities, they put their pride in their obedience, irrespective of what was asked of them, blinded by their faithfulness. During the trials that took place after the end of the war, most of them showed pride, not remorse at having executed orders even when these led to mass murders. The observers at the Eichmann trial were struck by the fact that he appeared frightfully normal, the perfect stereotype of the chronic adherent to mass movements. Hannah Arendt who wrote *Eichmann in Jerusalem* about the trial that she witnessed, sub-titled her book *A Report on the Banality of Evil.*

Cowardice and fear were also major determinants of the behavior of men during the French revolution and Nazi terror. The history of both periods is replete with stories of "honorable men" who let crimes be committed without intervening. The "terrorists" during the French revolution were themselves terrorized by whoever was in power in Paris at that point in time. Violence engendered fear, which brought terrorism. This spiral led men to execute others for fear of being executed themselves: Robespierre was eliminated by those who were afraid of being his next victims. Similarly, some of Hitler's officers blindly executed orders for fear that they and their families would pay the price of any perceived lack of absolute devotion to the Fuhrer.

FANATICISM AND TERRORISM

"Fanatic" and "terrorist" are now often used interchangeably even though throughout most of history they belonged to two worlds, which only partially overlapped.

Terrorism is based on the belief that acts of violence will transform the political, religious, or social landscape. The word was first coined, at the time of the French Revolution, by the "Directoire," in reference to the repression practiced by Robespierre. Historians say that the first terrorists were the Hashshashin, i.e. the Assassins, al-Hassan's Shia Muslim movement in the 11th century and the object of legends brought back by Marco Polo. From his fortress at Alamut in today's Iran, he would send fedayeen out into the Muslim world to kill for political or religious motivations. Later, the term qualified the activities of clandestine groups opposing the Tsar in Russia and the Emperors of the Austro-Hungarian Empire at the end of the 19th century. Since then, "terrorism" has taken many forms, ideological, state-led, or merely criminal (for example, in drug producing countries). At the beginning of the 21st century terrorist, exactions are widespread. They increasingly are committed by "suicide bombers," who not only take other people's lives in the name of some cause but also take their own, claiming a yearning for martyrdom.

There is no generally accepted definition of terrorism, and the gray areas are among others: must it be violent or have only recourse to the threat of violence? Must innocent people be targets? The UN has a long definition because the word can be applied to many different situations even as violence is always the predominant feature. It has different meanings for different people. It is well-known that "one man's terrorist is another man's freedom fighter." Anecdotally, at the Museum of the Army in Paris, in one of the rooms devoted to WWII, one can see posters printed by the Gestapo with the pictures and names of "terrorists." For the Allies, these men and women were "partisans" ready to give their lives to help liberate France.

The debate about a definition is not an academic one. Since September 11, 2001, most Western nations are leading a "war against terror" and as *The 9/11 Commission Report* pointed out, in order to fight terror efficiently, it matters to know who the adversaries are (Note 26). The disagreements about what to call the "quagmire" in Iraq in 2003 illustrate the weight that words carry. It is public knowledge (see *The New Yorker* dated 11/20/2006) that secretary Rumsfeld was adamant that the disturbances were caused by various isolated groups functioning like terrorists and never resolved to using the words "guerillas" and "insurgents." General Abizaid on the other hand believed that the coalition needed a coherent counter-insurgency strategy. How the situation was called reflected on how it was perceived and influenced how it was handled.

Scholars of terrorists define them as having a cause and using the threat of violence or actual violence to draw attention to their cause. Terrorists use violence as a means to communicate a message and with the expectation of forcing favorable changes. Historically, this has been the strategy of anarchists, nationalists, or religious groups.

Most terrorists are said to be blinded by their anger against what they perceive as the injustice committed against a group to which they belong. They identify with the interests of this group and kill (or threaten to kill) "for cause and comrade"; they are not sacrificing themselves for self-interest. There is little evidence that they are suffering from psychopathology. They inherit their cause from their family and peers: the majority of Protestants or Catholics in Northern Ireland who became terrorists did not choose their side. There are only a few instances of "hired terrorists," a well-known case being the Japanese Red Army Faction working for the Palestinians in 1972.

The difference between a true fanatic and a terrorist is the systematic recourse to violence by terrorists but also the pre-existence of a cause. It could be said that fanatics have a damaged personal identity which leads them to surrender themselves to a cause, while terrorists have a social identity which determines their cause.

This synoptic introduction to terrorism reflects a general understanding which has mostly been true up to the end of the 20th century. Many assertions could be questioned, starting with the motivations of the very people who gave terrorism its name. The "petits bourgeois," who joined the ranks of the revolutionaries in France in the 1790's and instituted "la Terreur" undoubtedly had the profile of "true believers" and used violence to impose their will, but what were their real motivations? Did they kill for a cause or to avoid being killed or more sordidly to get rid of enemies? Were they terrorists or fanatics turned criminals?

More importantly, since the end of the Cold War and the fortuitous concomitant emergence of the World Wide Web, the paths leading to acts of violence by many so-called terrorists no longer fit the historical model. In an age of globalized ideologies and communications, potential terrorists no longer need to be born with a cause and can join an ideological community physically dispersed but electronically connected.

This is illustrated by an article in the Jan, 22, 2007 edition of *The New Yorker* about "Azzam the American, The Making of an Al Qaeda Homegrown," by Raffi Khatchadourian. It tells the story of "Adam Gadahn, the first American to be charged with treason in more than fifty years." He was born in Oregon, grew up in rural California, converted to Islam at the age of seventeen, and became one of Osama bin Laden's senior operatives. The article refers to the empirical research about the process of Islamic radicalization described in *Understanding Terror Networks* (2004) by Marc Sageman.

Sageman had assembled the biographies of 172 Al Qaeda members and discovered that most operatives had been radicalized in the West and were from families that had solid middle and upper-middle class economic backgrounds.

Ideology and political grievances played a minimal role during the initial stages of enlistment. The future terrorists felt isolated, lonely, and alienated. These converts or "newly born Muslims" would congregate and form a closed society that they believed gave meaning to their life. Up to this point, the process is the one followed by every true fanatic. The radicalization of some men, as described by Sageman, was the result of "one-upmanship," members trying to outdo each other in the expression of their religious zeal. This suggested process of radicalization does not fully explain the passage for some from unconditionally endorsing a cause to having recourse to violence. This destiny is specific to each person.

These observations about the path followed by potential terrorists are confirmed by the analyses of the backgrounds of the men accused of committing the London attacks on July 7, 2005. As extensively reported in the press at the time, they were not poor or deprived but mostly directionless and confused about their identity. They did not want to share in the customs of their "new country," did not want to join those in Beeston, the Leeds neighborhood where they lived, who had fallen prey to drugs, alcohol, and crime. Islam gave them a cause and an identity, an "assertive and transnational identity" as the *New York Times* wrote on 7/31/2005. They joined without being recruited and self-radicalized.

It is noteworthy that doctrine did not play initially an important role for Sageman's operatives and the British bombers. This model diverges from the "historical" one, where the cause is present early on in the path followed by the terrorist. It might become more prevalent because, as E. Hoffer writes about the early adherents to mass movements,

"Our frustration is greater when we have much and want more than when we have nothing and want some."E.H

Widening acculturation and inequalities in opportunities rendered more visible by a quasi-universal access to information through the Internet are sources of such frustrations.

In *What Terrorists Want,* a book published in September 2006, Louise Richardson, a lecturer at Harvard, makes the point that all terrorist movements, and Al Qaeda in particular, require three components: alienated individuals, a legitimizing ideology, and a complicit community. This third feature has played historically an important role in the success of terrorism. Killing "for cause and comrade" takes place in environments which are favorable to the recourse to violence. Louis P. Pojman writes in *Terrorism and International Justice*:

> "Poverty and oppression are not sufficient (or even necessary) for terrorism, although they are contributing causes. The overriding impetus is a culture that endorses and reinforces violent responses against certain types of persons and property."

The cultures or ideological environments which encourage violence and condone terrorism open the door to the dehumanizing of the other. This, as we know, is an invitation for some people to destroy and kill in the name of their cause.

It is difficult to fight frustrated individuals who fanatically endorse a cause and live in communities who condone violence. People in charge of counter-terrorism explain that building intelligence networks, gathering information on potential terrorists, and isolating them from their community is the most effective strategy. It has worked in numerous cases. Louise Richardson analyzed the successful antiterrorism campaigns that have been waged since the end of the

Second World War and notes that they share a number of features. They were led by police intelligence and were aimed at separating the terrorists from their base in their community. This, it seems, can be an effective strategy when dealing with structured terrorist organizations. When any number of frustrated people can endorse a cause and kill in its name and they belong to scattered cells, as is the case of Al Qaeda, anticipating terrorist activity becomes a puzzle that has too many pieces.

One last reference on the topic of fighting terrorism. An anti-terrorist strategy successfully implemented in Yemen was based on the belief that terrorism has an intellectual theory behind it and any kind of intellectual idea can be defeated by intellect. Just as militants of extremists movements have been led astray, so too can they be taught more moderate ideas.

The anatomy of true fanatics reveals people who joined a movement for the comfort that it brought them, not for what it stood for. In other words, their need for identity, belonging, and certitudes could be satisfied by any number of causes. They believe in the superiority of the truths that they have reached. The "true believers" dehumanize those who do not share these beliefs and eventually eliminate them. The analyses of the most recent form of terrorist acts indicate that they were committed by people who followed a similar path. They converted to a cause or surrendered their self to one that might have been a dormant part of their identities. They were led to commit criminal acts when convinced by their peers that nonbelievers were impure and unworthy. These terrorists are not different from true believers. This means that over the long term, the fight against terrorism is not a fight against a cause. It cannot be a fight against the reasons of frustrations which are more the result of psychological needs than material want. It requires offering models of communities that people can join and which would reflect positively on their lives. The war against terror should be the fight of hope against despair. In order to win, the defenders of the rights and dignity of man must be as fanatic in their beliefs as the fanatics and terrorists that they fight. Giving hope and remembering that every human is worthy of esteem are the two keys to a successful battle.

⚓ ⚓ ⚓

NOTE 23

The concept of pseudo-transcendence used herein is taken from *Psychology of Terrorism* by Chris Stout.

NOTE 24

Obedience may be a deeply ingrained behavior tendency, an impulse overriding training in ethics. The psychologist Stanley Milgram devised a procedure to study destructive obedience. The experiment was conducted at Yale University in 1961. It was destined to throw light on the process of obedience from the sociopsychological standpoint. The salient features of this well known experiment are the following:

Naive subjects called teachers would ask questions to a learner (a trained confederate of the experimenter). After each wrong answer, the teachers would be commanded by the experimenter to administer increasingly more intense electric shocks. The instrument panel used by the naive subjects indicated a range from fifteen to 450 volts. The learner would signal his pain when the level reached three hundred by pounding on the wall of the room in which he was bound to a makeshift electric chair and, as the shock level is further increased, would become silent. Whenever a teacher would indicate his unwillingness to go on, the experimenter would use a sequence of prods, as many as necessary to bring the naive subject into line.

Contrary to all predictions, twenty-six out of forty continued to the highest level of 450 volts. The other fourteen refused to obey the commands at various stages when the level reached three hundred volts.

The other finding, besides the strength of obedient tendencies, was the extreme tension generated in the teachers by the procedure.

Milgram's experiment has stirred much controversy. Its dramatic conclusions have often been referenced but have also been questioned.

NOTE 25

A mixed population of what in England was termed "lower order" was called in France in the 1790's, "sans culottes" (i.e. without culottes). The term literally refers to the wearing of pants instead of knee-length culottes and silk stockings. The outfit of manual workers and specifically the long pants were adopted by the revolutionaries and became a symbol of the "citizens."

NOTE 26

Abstract from "The 9/11 Commission Report":
"But the enemy is not just 'terrorism,' some generic evil. This vagueness blurs the strategy. The catastrophic threat at this moment in history is more specific. It is the threat posed by Islamist terrorism— especially the al Qaeda network, its affiliates and its ideology."

Also:
"…effective public policies also need concrete objectives. Vague goals match an amorphous picture of the enemy."

CONCLUDING REMARKS

"Nothing great in the world has been accomplished without passion."
Philosophy of History by Friedrich Hegel.

Sports fans and fanatics look for an identity and seek features that single them out; they have a need to belong, to be part of a community; they yearn to express their feelings, emotions, and passions. This can be achieved when they are enthusiastically committed to a cause, a team, or something else. What is true for sports fans can be true for fanatics at a higher level of intensity.

And this is well and good as long as they respect the physical and mental space of others, do not surrender to all their emotions just because they are theirs, do not maintain that all their ideas are just and reasonable, and keep questioning their belief that there is only one horizon, one absolute truth.

We know that in their search for acknowledgment and belonging, men do not always follow these rules. Some will do anything to fill the void of their lives; they can become hooligans, true believers, and terrorists.

We know that being a sport fan can be a pretext for racism and other forms of xenophobia, and it can lead to cold-blooded and scripted violence and breakdowns in civility. These are the highly visible unpleasant aspects of sport fandom.

However, its social benefits far outweigh these negatives. Sport fandom can offer non-threatening sources of identity and belonging to people and can help mend the social fabric.

Is it utopian to wonder if becoming the passionate fans of a team or athlete might provide enough of an identity and sense of belonging to help communities steer clear of the dangerous reef of ideological certainty? When Iraq's national soccer team won the 2007 Asian cup, a squad of Sunnis, Shiites, and Kurds gave Iraqis a rare occasion to celebrate as one nation.

The more tribes of people are enthusiastic about something for its own sake, the less they might look for absolutes or surrender to the pressure to be acknowledged at any cost.

This book started with a page from World War II and will end with a moment taken from World War I.

On Christmas Day 1914, the first Christmas of a tragic war, in some areas along the front in the North of France, foes called a truce. For one day, they dealt with each other as human beings, and they did what men from England, France and Germany did best when together, they shared wine and songs and played soccer. They sang Christmas carols, uncorked bottles, and played. Soccer games played by foes in no-man's lands between the trenches on Christmas day, men united for a short moment by sport. There would be a price to pay by those poor souls who had ventured into a moment of sanity, but I will end the story on the marvelous image of these young men finding peace and recapturing their humanity in this other world, the world of sport.

The game is on; time to close the book; go Raiders/ Arsenal/Red Sox, go all the teams that have entered and enhanced our lives.

Appendix 1
NICOLAS COPERNICUS and GALILEO GALILEI

Nicolas Copernicus, born in 1473 in Poland, was a church canon, who devoted his free time to his passion, astronomy. He fell under the spell of heliocentrism, the concept that the earth revolves around the sun. Such an assumption went against the long held belief that the earth was the center of the universe. He dreamed of demonstrating the validity of the heliocentric idea using mathematical models. As he was struggling to construct a system, he took great care to remain silent about the concept and kept tirelessly working at a monumental work, *De revolutionibus orbum coelestium* (The Revolutions of the Heavenly Spheres). He did agree to the publication of his work in 1543, but when the first copy was given to him, he was on his death bed.

To this day, it remains a matter of conjecture why he finally went public. Even though the foreword of his book says that the concept, as presented, is an assumption, Copernicus knew that he was treading on dangerous ground. If man was no longer at the center of the universe, the Catholic religion, i.e. Rome, would feel threatened. It also must be remembered that the Council of Trent had prohibited the interpretation of the Scripture contrary to the common agreement of the Holy Fathers, all of whom understood the Bible to state clearly that the Sun traveled around the world.

Even though he was firmly convinced of the truth of heliocentrism, Copernicus, the believer, did not convince his contemporaries. His mathematical demonstration might have been too weak, and his pursuit too solitary to support a concept that was so revolutionary for its time.

Other men played a role in the introduction of new concepts in astronomy in the 16th century, and a prominent figure was Galileo.

Galileo Galilei was born in 1564 in Pisa, Italy. Like Copernicus, he was passionate about astronomy. He made numerous observations using a telescope that he had built and became a believer in the heliocentric system hypothesized by Copernicus. As early as 1610, he considered writing a book on the "systems of the world." He assumed that if he presented his ideas ex hypothesi, i.e. based on assumptions, he could venture with new concepts. He knew that as long as he lacked serious proof, it would be too dangerous to call heliocentrism a truth. Giordano Bruno, who had spread ideas on the universe that had been unacceptable to the Church, had been burned at the stake, in Rome, in 1600! In 1616, Copernicus's work was banned by the Church, and the Holy Office forbid Galileo to teach the theories of Copernicus.

Encouraged by the election of a liberal pope, Galileo decided to write a master work, which would attempt to remain neutral between the heliocentric and the geocentric systems. His poor health tempered his enthusiasm, and the manuscript was finished only in 1629. The book was printed in 1632 and is known by the title of *Dialogues*. Distribution was immediately stopped because the work could be interpreted as a defense of heliocentrism, which was actually what Galileo wanted to achieve and in the political atmosphere at the time, Pope Urban VIII could not afford to be perceived as lax with ideas that went against Catholic doctrine. Galileo was summoned to appear before the Pope in September 1632. He was accused by the Inquisition of having violated the prohibition to defend Copernicus' theory. In June 1633, he was found guilty of heresy. Legend has it that when he kneeled and publicly admitted his mistake, he murmured "eppu, si muove" (but still it moves). He was sentenced to life in prison, which the Pope changed to house arrest. He stayed in his villa outside of Florence up to his death in 1642.

With the benefit of hindsight it can be said that Galileo's demonstration of heliocentrism was weak, and scientific confirmation would come many years later (for example, Foucault proved in 1851 that the earth rotates around its axis). Galileo used faith to reach a truth that few others believed in. He should be remembered as much for the tenacity with which he implemented a scientific approach as for his contribution to astronomy. He led a passionate defense of the position of science in the world.

Copernicus, presumably because he felt less confident about his demonstration of heliocentrism, remained prudent up to his last days. Galileo, more self assured, behaved with the stubbornness of a passionate fanatic. Those who followed the way he had paved would define the world as we understand it today. The heretics would become the orthodox.

EUGENE DUBOIS

The following biography is based on Pat Shipman's excellent book *The Man Who Found The Missing Link*.

Eugene Dubois was born in 1858 in the southeastern corner of Holland. An event with momentous consequences on his life took place a few years later, the publishing by Charles Darwin of *The Origin of Species*. At the age of ten, he heard a German biologist, Karl Vogt, speak on the evolutionary theory. This view of the history of the world as dynamic, marked by struggle and competition, was menacing for many at the time. Dubois, though, was attracted by the new theory's ability to upset the old order as well as by its sheer scientific power; he adopted it with an almost religious fervor. When he turned twelve, his father granted him his wish to go to technical high school. There, he read Haeckel's *History of Creation*. He became an evolutionist. He adopted Haeckel's theory that there is a link as yet unknown between apes and man and so began his life long passion, the discovery of fossils of this "missing link" (the expression comes from an image which compares the creatures of the earth to links on a chain). He started to study medicine at the University of Amsterdam at the age of nineteen and four years later, in 1881, accepted an assistantship in anatomy at the same University. Years passed, bringing him closer to the position of professor of anatomy when, in 1888, the finding of Neanderthal fossils in Spy (Belgium) awakened the passion of his adolescence for evolution and his belief that only the fossil remains of the transitional form between ape and man can prove evolution irrefutably. He set his mind to find our long lost ancestor.

Where to look for something more ape like, more primitive than a Neanderthal? He focused on Asia, not Africa, because gibbons are the apes most akin to humans, and they are Asian animals. He read everything he could find relating to the topic, looked for clues in paleontology, geology, natural history. His logical analyses led him to conclude that Sumatra was the place where he should look for fossilized remains of the missing link. He enlisted as a military surgeon in the Dutch colonial army and in October 1887 sailed with his wife Anna and daughter, Eugenie, for the Indies, where he intended to carry on his quest.

Let us pause at this juncture to reflect on the power of passion. Here we have a man who believes he sees the truth clearly and puts his future at stake on the strength of his conviction. What was the probability of finding specific fossils? Infinitesimal. Nevertheless, he gambled his life and that of his family for the sake of his passion, to prove evolution.

In Sumatra, he delivered his first son in June 1888, caught malaria with which he would battle repeatedly, and despite adventurous digging expeditions made few worthwhile discoveries besides some fossil apes and gibbons in a cave called Lida Adjer, at the end of the year. He decided that he might have more luck on the island of Java. He set sail for Batavia in the middle of 1890 and settled in east Java. He realized rapidly that because of the local topography his chances would be much improved if he searched in riverbeds instead of caves. By the middle of 1891, he had the intuition to dig in a river next to the village of Trinil. Almost immediately, he found a tooth that must have belonged to something nearly human; in October, he found a skullcap, and then in august 1892, a long femur. The skullcap had too big a braincase for an ape and the femur was undoubtedly from a large animal that walked on two legs like a man. Both came from the same geologic stratum. There was a lot of ape in the skull, and a lot of man in the femur. He started a frantic working schedule, compared the skulls of a gibbon, a human, and a chimp to that of the fossil and became convinced that he had found the missing link. Borrowing from Ernst Haeckel he called it « Pithecanthropus erectus » (P.e.). He had to let the scientific world know about his discovery and set about writing a monograph. The manuscript was finished in late 1893. At the end of his tour of duty in June 1895, he left Java to return to Holland.

This should have been his finest hour, but it was not to be. First, disaster struck his family. His father died in April 1893. He had had such great hope to earn his father's approval by making a great discovery. Then in August that year, Anna was delivered of a stillborn fetus. The couple didn't survive this drama. A few years later, Dubois would end up living apart from his wife. More crushing, even, his discovery met with a lot of skepticism in the scientific world. Instead of being honored, he was criticized and accused of foolishness and incompetence. He should have expected the resistance which accompanies new things. He knew that anything to do with human evolution was very controversial. Nevertheless, as much as he had been ready to accept failure in his search, he could not accept to have his success unjustly ignored. This marked the beginning of a life of anguish and solitude.

Up to his death, he would fight and always fight to prove to the scientific world that the apelike skull and the human-like femur were from the missing link. These fossils would become more important to him than anything or anyone else. He grew hypersensitive, over protective of his work, always expecting betrayal. He moved from a man of passion, committed to the truth that he believed in to a fanatic, obsessive, more and more rigid, less and less tolerant. The privations of war put an end to his struggles when he died in December 1940.

"P.e. had been his life, his great discovery, his tribute to Science and Truth."

He had been a "modern Galileo."

Appendix 2

Le BON and CROWD PSYCHOLOGY

Crowd psychology became a component of social psychology at the end of the 19th century. The social thinkers who left their imprint on this discipline are Hippolyte Taine (1828–1893), Gabriel Tarde (1843–1904), and Gustave Le Bon (1841–1931). Sigmund Freud also brought his contribution.

Crowd psychology is concerned with the contrast between the behavior of individuals and that of gatherings of people.

Crowds had a negative image at the turn of the 20th century, presumably as a result of the numerous social upheavals which were shaking Europe. In order to explain the behavior of individuals forming a crowd, the above mentioned psychologists used concepts such as "suggestion," "hypnosis," "imitation." Le Bon, and later on Freud, stressed the predominance of the unconscious. Such an approach was slowly abandoned during the 20th century as the importance of individuals was stressed. Also, social psychology, "a la Francaise," was slowly replaced by group psychology dear to American academics. It should be noted that *Crowd Psychology*, the book written by Le Bon in 1895, was regularly reissued, and more than 110 years after its first publication, it is still generally considered as the primo inter pares reference on the topic. One reason often given for this longevity is that some politicians appreciate one of the concepts posited by Le Bon, i.e. that the irrational behavior of crowds can be avoided by good leadership (which can be interpreted as: vote for me and you will have social peace) and also because ultra-conservatives were keen to present patriotism as a means to channel mass passions.

What distinguishes a crowd from a group is its degree of organization, the type of interaction between people and, more generally, how "being together" is perceived. One of the consequences of the low level of organization in crowds is that they are unpredictable and consequently can be frightening.

Here are some of Le Bon's statements:

-individuals forming a crowd share a collective mentality.

-the identity of individuals forming a crowd becomes an unconscious identity; they are not themselves anymore.

-men in a crowd revert to "barbaric" behavior; they exhibit the spontaneity, the violence, the ferocity but also the enthusiasm and heroic behavior of primitive beings.

-the feelings of a crowd are simplistic and amplified; because of the certitude of impunity and the feeling of temporary power given by the mass, people in a crowd can behave in manners which are unacceptable for individuals on their own; crowds are easily influenced and are credulous.

Even as Le Bon's image among academics has faded and his approach has been criticized, whenever the topic is "crowd psychology," one can expect to read a paraphrase of any of the above views.

Made in the USA
Lexington, KY
11 September 2012